BRITAIN IN OLD ... APHS

EALING, HANWELL & GREENFORD

RICHARD ESSEN

SUTTON PUBLISHING LIMITED

Sutton Publishing Limited
Phoenix Mill · Thrupp · Stroud
Gloucestershire · GL5 2BU

First published 1997

Page 1: main entrance to the Hoover Building, Perivale, *c*. 1935.

British Library Cataloguing in Publication Data
A catalogue record for this book is available from the British Library.

ISBN 0-7509-1674-5

Typeset in 10/12 Perpetua.
Typesetting and origination by
Sutton Publishing Limited.
Printed in Great Britain by
Ebenezer Baylis, Worcester.

To Vicky

Fan-tailed doves and peacocks in Walpole Park, Ealing, *c*. 1903.

CONTENTS

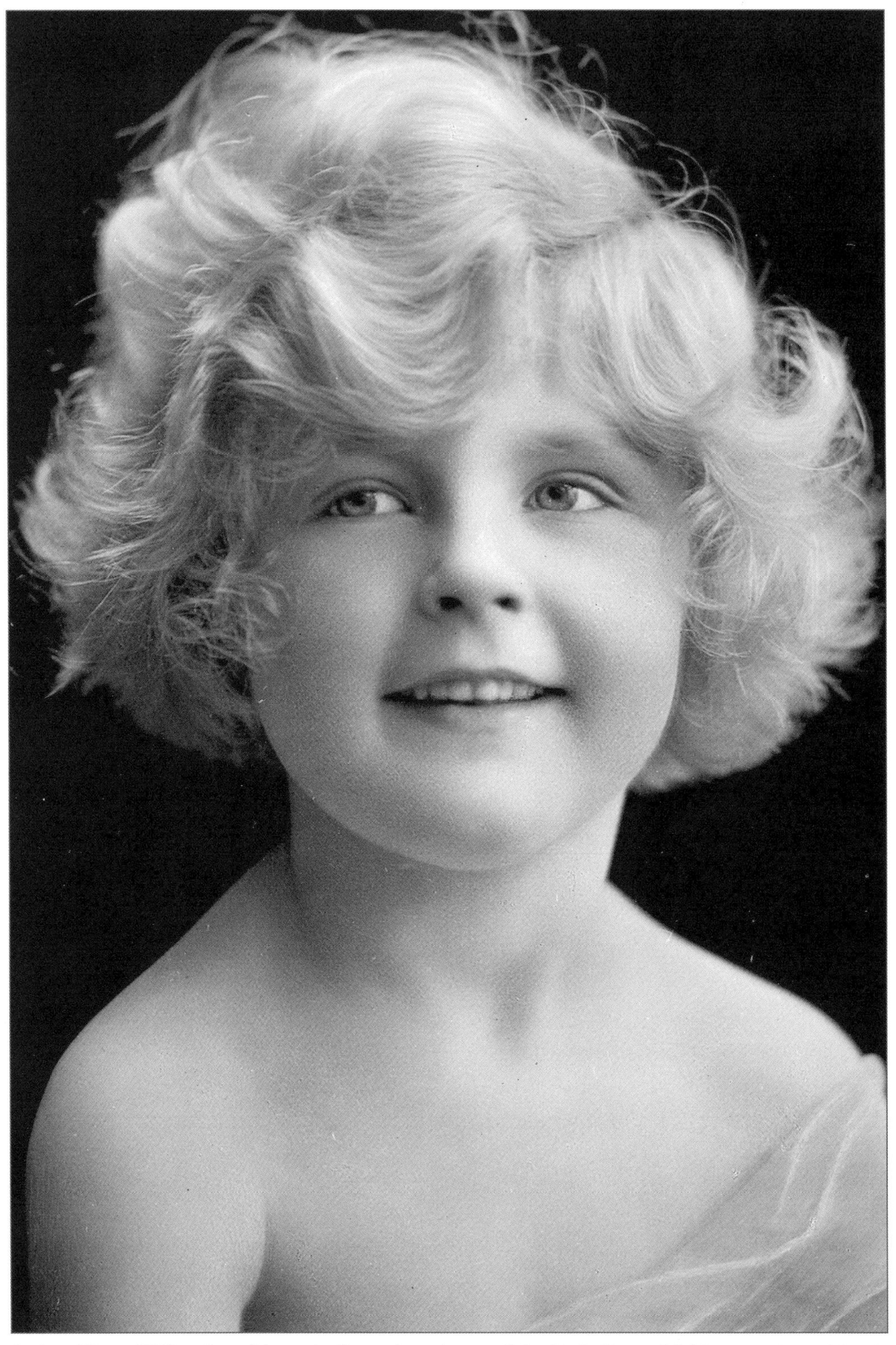

Audrey King of Ealing (age 4½ years), first prize winner of the *Daily Mirror* child beauty competition in 1923.

INTRODUCTION

Ealing, Hanwell and Greenford is more than an examination of Ealing, after which the London borough is named. In three chapters, each area is illustrated in rich photographs spanning the twentieth century. Among the detached villas which helped Ealing become the 'Queen of the Suburbs' are the large country houses, including Sir John Soane's Pitshanger Manor and the Rothschild's Gunnersbury Park.

Hanwell was not as fashionable as Ealing because of the institutional buildings, the Asylum and the Cuckoo Schools, and the cemeteries built near its boundaries. This is reflected by the former estate of Hanwell Park, which no longer survives. Perhaps one of Hanwell's most impressive buildings is the church of St Thomas, designed by Sir Edward Maufe, who also designed Guildford Cathedral.

The Greenford chapter includes sections on Perivale, Twyford and Northolt. At Greenford, estate building was dominated by two families, the Ravenors and the Costons. Ravenor Park estate was the first to be constructed, on the site of Ravenor Farm, and this marked the beginning of the end for other farms in the area, which were bought up for housing purposes. Greenford Road and Western Avenue provided a network of roads around which the house building continued in the 1930s.

There are some interesting pictures of the famous Hoover building at Perivale and the estate around it, sponsored by Sir Percy Bilton. The next section shows the transition of Twyford, from the days when Twyford Abbey dominated the parish to the development of Park Royal, at the beginning of the 1900s, and the Hanger Lane gyratory system. The final Northolt section illustrates the progression from the farms of the twenties to the residential estates of the post-war period. All these areas are included in the London Borough of Ealing that we know today.

Richard Essen
1997

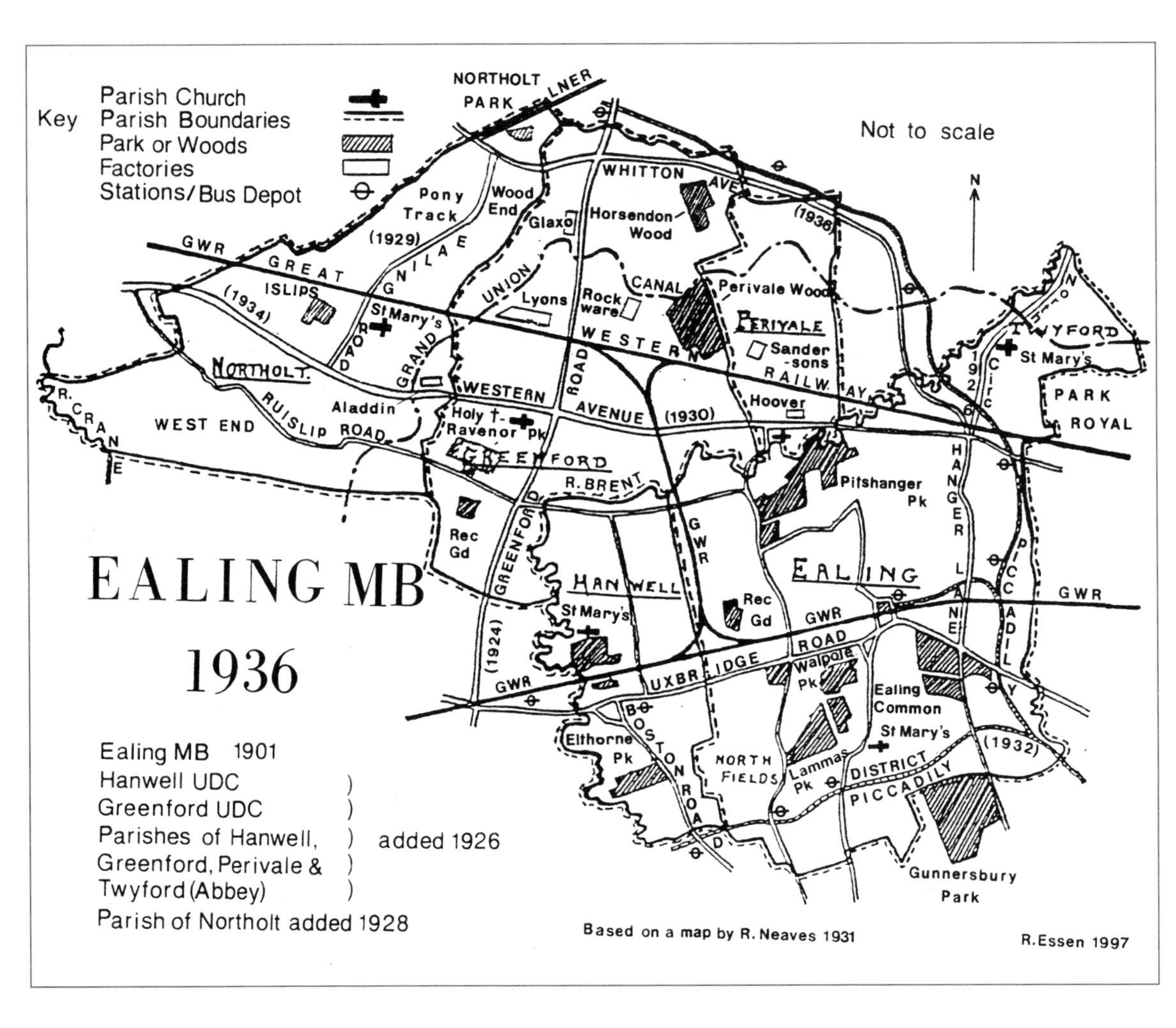
Key
Parish Church
Parish Boundaries
Park or Woods
Factories
Stations/Bus Depot
Not to scale
N
EALING MB
1936
Ealing MB 1901
Hanwell UDC)
Greenford UDC)
Parishes of Hanwell,) added 1926
Greenford, Perivale &)
Twyford (Abbey))
Parish of Northolt added 1928
NORTHOLT PARK
LNER
WHITTON AVE
(1936)
Pony Track
(1929)
Wood End
Glaxo
Horsendon Wood
GWR
GREAT ISLIPS
(1934)
St Mary's
UNION
GRAND
CANAL
Lyons
Rock ware
Perivale Wood
PERIVALE
Sander -sons
WESTERN
RAILWAY
NORTHOLT
R. CRANE
WEST END
RUISLIP ROAD
Aladdin
WESTERN AVENUE (1930)
Holy †- Ravenor pk
Hoover
GREENFORD
R. BRENT
TWYFORD
St Mary's
PARK ROYAL
HANGER LANE
Pitshanger Pk
Rec Gd
HANWELL
St Mary's
GWR
Rec Gd
EALING
GWR
(1924)
GWR
UXBRIDGE ROAD
Walpole Pk
Ealing Common
St Mary's
PICCADILLY
(1932)
Elthorne Pk
BOSTON ROAD
NORTH FIELDS
Lammas Pk
DISTRICT
PICCADILY
Gunnersbury Park
Based on a map by R. Neaves 1931
R.Essen 1997

SECTION ONE

EALING

Greetings from Ealing, with views of the new corporation buildings, *c.* 1905.

The earliest settlement was around St Mary's Parish Church, at the Brentford end of Ealing. Gunnersbury Park and Pitshanger Manor were the large country houses. The arrival of the Great Western Railway in 1838 helped to move the business centre to Uxbridge Road. The real suburban growth was fostered when Charles Jones of Ealing Urban District Council laid down the infrastructure of Ealing in Kentish ragstone. This and the arrival of the District Railway in 1878, with its connection to London, attracted the middle classes and Ealing became 'Queen of the Suburbs'. In 1901, after much opposition, the working classes were provided with trams along the Uxbridge Road which linked to a new estate at Northfields. This transport provision contributed to an increase in Ealing's population, from 3,031 in 1901 to 61,222 in 1911. The middle classes were also catered for, with Ealing's Garden Suburb at Brentham built during the period 1905 to 1911. In the twenties and thirties new estates were built on Hanger Hill, Gunnersbury Avenue and Western Avenue (the Greystoke estate). The Central and Piccadilly Lines were extended to serve the new estates. These transport links radiating into the newly built-up areas allowed Ealing to spread its influence. In 1926 Hanwell and Greenford were absorbed into the Metropolitan Borough of Ealing, and Northolt followed in 1928.

Ealing Broadway station, *c.* 1900. The first station was opened by the Great Western Railway in 1838. The rail motor car is probably on the route to Greenford via the Castlebar loop. Ealing Theatre is on the right.

Ealing Broadway with Ealing Theatre on the right, *c.* 1915. The Lyric Hall had opened in 1887 but in 1899 the Ealing Theatre and Lyric Restaurant were built on the site. In 1912 it was renamed the Ealing Hippodrome and housed the Palladium Cinema from 1914 to 1958. Opposite, on the left, is a bank; the building behind it opened in 1883.

The Town Hall, Uxbridge Road, *c.* 1900. Designed by Charles Jones in Kentish ragstone, it was built at a cost of £21,000 and replaced the smaller offices on the Mall. Prince Edward and Princess Alexandra opened it on 15 December 1888. Jones also designed the Old Fire House (1888) and the Victoria Hall (1889).

Broadway and Spring Bridge Road, *c.* 1904. Eldred Sayers & Son drapers' shop opened in 1837. The domed extension was added in 1902 after the arrival of the trams in 1901 which brought shoppers in from West Ealing, Hanwell, Acton and Shepherds Bush. Today Sayers has been demolished and the Waterglade Centre now occupies the site.

The library, Walpole Park, seen here *c.* 1924, was the former Pitshanger Manor. The outstanding architect at the turn of the nineteenthth century was Sir John Soane. His earliest work in Middlesex, during 1788–9, was his additions to Bentley Priory for the Marquess of Abercorn. In 1800 Soane settled in Pitshanger Manor, Ealing. The south wing was built by George Dance the Younger in 1770, to which Soane added the centre portion in 1802 for his own residence as a country villa. The house demonstrates typical Soane trademarks, such as arches and Ionic columns outside, and enfilade rooms and symmetry inside. The use of colour at Ealing provides a striking contrast with his town house at Lincoln's Inn Fields, where Sir John Soane's Museum is situated.

Entrance to the library and Walpole Park, *c.* 1919. Soane's north-east gateway also has an eccentric mix of materials, rubbed red brick with pilaster strips of knapped flint and stone top-hampers of typical Soanic outline. The triumphal arch theme of the Pitshanger front was echoed by Norwood Hall (built 1801–03). Pitshanger Manor was bought as the library in 1902. In 1984 the library moved to the Broadway Centre and the building became Pitshanger Museum and has been restored with a Soane interior.

The bridge, Walpole Park, *c.* 1904. The serpentine lake north-west of the house was bounded at the north end by a picturesque three-arched bridge designed by Soane in 1802, and built of flint and cyclopean masonry. The lake was replanted as a sunken garden in the 1920s. Soane's work can also be found at Aynscombe, Harden Hewish, Letton Hall stables and Sourbrook.

Mayor's Walk in Walpole Park is so named because it is lined by an avenue of trees, each one commemorating a Mayor's year of office. Walpole Park was opened to the public on 1 May 1901 by the Right Honourable George Hamilton, MP for Ealing and Secretary of State of India. It was bought by the Ealing District Council in 1899 from Sir Spencer Walpole KCB for £40,000, with one-quarter paid by Middlesex County Council.

Ealing County School for boys, Ealing Green, *c.* 1920. The school was built in 1913 by H.G. Crothall, an architect for Middlesex County Council, in an early eighteenth-century style of red brick with a stone centrepiece. Extensions were added in 1936, 1961 and 1964. Ealing County School for girls was opened at The Park, Ealing.

Ealing County School for boys, Ealing Green, *c.* 1920. It became Ealing Green High School and changed again to Ealing Tertiary College in 1992.

Disraeli Road, Ealing. The road ran alongside George Barker's studios, which he set up in 1904 at West Lodge, Ealing Green. The enterprise became the largest film studio in Britain by 1912 and was the forerunner of Ealing Film Studios. On the other side of Disraeli Road were Cairn Avenue and St Nicholas Gardens, which were built in 1908 on the site of Great Ealing School.

St Mary's Road, Ealing *c.* 1913, with the General's 65 bus just passing Sunnyside Road. On the left are shop nos 12 to 20.

High Street, Ealing, *c.* 1900. The tall building between the spire of Christ Church and the tree belonged to Lamertons, a furniture removal business which is now the Photographer and Firkin pub. The shops on the right include that of S. Woodcock, and a horse-drawn cart from Hounslow is making a delivery.

High Street, Ealing, *c.* 1900. On the right the shops include Reeve, C.W. Pitt, a picture liner and restorer, Smith Ambrose, a hosier, and Teetgen & Co. Ltd, tea merchants. On the right is Ealing Green, which was overlooked by the library, the former Pitshanger Manor.

High Street and Bond Street Parade, Ealing, *c.* 1911. High Street is to the right and Bond Street Parade to the left. Bond Street Parade and Sandringham Parade were built in 1905 when a new road, Bond Street, was laid out cutting through residential housing on Sandringham Gardens.

Ealing Green and High Street, Ealing, *c.* 1916. This parade of shops was built in 1902 at the junction of High Street and The Grove. The shop on the corner is Ealing Bon Marché.

The Grove, Ealing, *c.* 1910. The Grove was known as Love Lane until the 1890s. Its new name was taken from Ealing Grove House, which was bought by Lady Byron in 1834 for use as a school. When Ealing Grove House was demolished in 1894, houses and shops were built on the site to serve the new residents. Henry Beer's tobacconist shop of 1894, on the corner with Western Road, is now a wine and coffee bar. The Kings Arms with its jolly corner turret, just out of view, was opened in 1897.

Grange Park, Ealing, *c.* 1921. In 1864 the area where Grange Park is situated was still covered by fields. There was a house called The Grange on Grange Road, which gave its name to the new area of Grange Park.

Grange Park, Ealing, *c.* 1921. This housing development was built in a T shape within a box formed by The Common, Grange, Warwick and Kenilworth Roads. In the middle of the T was a small green.

Byron Road, Ealing Common, *c.* 1907. Byron Road and Fordhook Avenue were built on the site of Fordhook. The road is named after Lady Lord Byron (1792–1860), who lived in Fordhook after she was separated from her husband, Lord Byron, the poet, in 1816. Lord Byron left England for Greece, where he wrote *Don Juan* and where he died in 1824. Lady Byron is commemorated by a blue plaque on the outside of Thames Valley University marking the site of the Co-operative School.

Wolverton Mansions, Uxbridge Road, Ealing Common, *c.* 1910. These flats were built almost opposite Ealing Common station, which the District Railway opened on 1 July 1879. The flats were built in the early 1900s between Wolverton Gardens and Hanger Lane.

Hanger Lane, Ealing Common, *c.* 1919. Hanger Lane led to Hanger Hill Golf Club and Fox Reservoir. This narrow lane became a feeder for the North Circular, which opened in 1926, and Western Avenue, which opened in 1928. The narrowness of Hanger Lane was addressed in the sixties when a plan was put forward to build a road underneath Ealing Common. This was stopped though because the trees either side of the Common were protected; if the road had been built underneath it would have damaged their roots.

Hanger Hill Golf Club, *c.* 1915. Built in 1790, Hanger Hill House was let by the Wood estate to Sir Edward Montague Nelson between 1874 and 1901 and was opened by him as the headquarters of Hanger Hill Golf Club in 1901. It was let as a golf club between 1901 and 1930. Sir Edward came to Ealing from Warwickshire and was the Charter Mayor in 1901. The site of the golf club was sold and developed as the Hanger Hill estate by Haymills Ltd from 1933 (see pp. 116–17).

Fox Reservoir, Hillcrest Road, Ealing, seen here in *c.* 1910, was built on the site of Mount Castle, which was said to have been an Elizabethan watch-tower. The reservoir was opened by Edward G. Fox, Chairman of Grand Junction Waterworks, on 3 August 1888, and held 50 million gallons of water. It was bought by Ealing Council in 1949 and is now Fox Wood in Hanger Hill Park.

Ealing Grammar School, The Park, *c.* 1906. Lady Byron opened a private boys' school in Ealing Grove House in 1834. Charles Atlee moved it to The Park and it was known as Byron House School until 1901 when it became Ealing Grammar School. It had closed by 1928 and the rest of the land was bought in 1929 for Ealing County Girls' School, which is now owned by Thames Valley University. The main school buildings are shown on the right, with an entrance off The Park. These are now private houses. Edwardian houses, facing Kerrison Road, were built on the spot where the photographer was standing. The school's iron chapel still remains and is privately owned.

Liverpool Road, Ealing, *c.* 1934. The Rectory estate was bought in the 1850s by the Conservative Freehold Land Society. Liverpool, Ranelagh, Blandford, Marlborough and Richmond Roads were laid out by the mid-1860s. Many of the houses were built between 1862 and 1868.

Ealing Carnival Queens: Lucy Davis in a pale green train (1908), Nora Gabilies in old gold (1909), May Curtis in pale pink (1910), Winnie Burville in pale mauve (1911), Winnie Ducat in dark green (1912), Amy Harrison in a white train (1913), Kathleen Hayter in a pink train (1914), Winnie Taylor in a white embroidery train (1916).

Henry Chandler, bootmaker, with his wife and daughter, 6 South Ealing Road, *c.* 1913. It is now Patrick Ryan and Daughter, Funeral Services.

St Mary's, Ealing, *c.* 1910. St Mary's was the old parish church of Ealing around which the village of Ealing grew until the arrival of the Great Western Railway in 1838, whereupon the business centre transferred to Haven Green and Uxbridge Road. The medieval parish church was rebuilt between 1735 and 1740 and enlarged between 1866 and 1874 by S.S. Teulon in Early French Gothic style as a 'Constantinopolitan Basilica'. Teulon's other work in Middlesex included the vicarage of St John the Baptist at Hampton Wick in 1854, Holy Trinity at Northwood in 1854, Hanworth Park rectory in 1865 and St George, Hanworth, rebuilt in 1865.

St Mary's Road, Ealing, *c.* 1911. Long and Pocock's Dairy is in the parade of shops on the right.

Esmond Gardens, St Mary's Road, Ealing, *c.* 1911. Long and Pocock had a head office at West Ealing and branches at Northfields, Hanwell, Brentford, Acton and Chiswick. Long and Pocock Dairies were taken over by United Dairies in the twenties.

A bus on route 65 on St Mary's Road, South Ealing, *c.* 1913. The New Inn on the left dates from the seventeenth century and was originally a coaching stage post when the Ives family ran a coaching service to London. The inn's extensive stable yard is now part of St Mary's Court next door. In the nineteenth century a corridor connected the inn to the Hall of Variety or Assembly Rooms, which were Ealing's venue for public entertainment until the Lyric Hall was built on the Uxbridge Road in 1887. The pub was rebuilt in 1897. In the 1980s the New Inn Theatre was active in a first-floor room until the curtain was brought down for the last time in 1985.

Convent of Nazareth de Montléan, Little Ealing Lane, 1901. In 1882 William Lawrence, the owner of the Ealing Park estate, sold the land to the British Land Company for housing development, and the house was sold as a Roman Catholic convent. The first order to occupy it was the Sisters of Nazareth. In 1903 they passed it on to the Little Sisters of Charity, who occupied it as St Anne's High School until it closed in 1987. It was rebuilt in 1988–9 and is now the King Fahad Academy for Girls.

Little Ealing Lane, South Ealing. The other convent on Little Ealing Lane was the Convent of the Sacred Heart of Mary, Lourdes Mount, which opened in 1923.

Robert Castrey outside his gent's outfitters' shop, 145 and 147 South Ealing Road, *c*. 1923. It is now A and B Candy Stores and Post Office.

Pope's Lane, South Ealing, *c*. 1921. The road was named after Alexander Pope, the eighteenth-century poet who wrote the *Dunciad* in 1726 and *An Essay on Man* in 1733. He died in Twickenham in 1744. There was a memorial to Pope at the cross-roads with South Ealing Road but now the only marker is Pope's Lane.

Gunnersbury Park main entrance, Pope's Lane, with Barons Pond outside, *c.* 1928. Lionel Nathan de Rothschild, who lived at Gunnersbury Park, was invited to the first run of the trams through Ealing and formally opened them on 10 July 1901. Outside the gates are a delivery bicycle and carts. Gunnersbury Park Mansion had large kitchens which were supplied by the local shops. The Mansion had thirty staff including coachmen and footmen as well as the kitchen staff.

Gunnersbury Park Mansion main lawns and horseshoe pond, *c.* 1919. The park was opened to the public in 1926 by the Minister of Health, Neville Chamberlain. The clay lining of the horseshoe pond was damaged by bombs during the Second World War, causing the water to leak out and the clay lining to dry up. After the war the pond was filled in and, in the late 1960s, a rockery was laid out at the western end of the dried out pond.

GUNNERSBURY PARK

In the fifteenth century the estate belonged to the Frowick family. During 1658–63 John Webb built a house here for Sir John Maynard, Charles II's law adviser. Princess Amelia, daughter of George II, used the house as her summer residence from 1763 to 1768. The original Gunnersbury House was demolished in 1801 and the estate was split in two. The two mansions which replaced the former house were called Gunnersbury Park Mansion,built in 1802, and Gunnersbury House, built in 1806. In 1835 Nathan Mayer Rothschild bought Gunnersbury Park Mansion. In 1836 Sydney Smirke altered the Mansion and added the orangery and stables, and John Claudius Loudon improved the entrance. Nathan Mayer died before it was completed and Lionel Nathan de Rothschild, who became the first Jewish Member of Parliament, inherited it in 1836. It passed to Leopold de Rothschild in 1879 and in 1889 he bought Gunnersbury House for his guests. He lived here until 1917 when part of the estate was sold for building. After Leopold died in 1925, the two houses and 186-acre estate were bought by the Borough Councils of Ealing and Acton for sports and recreation purposes. In 1927 the Urban District of Brentford and Chiswick agreed to join in owning and managing the park. In 1965 the estate was transferred to the new London Boroughs of Ealing and Hounslow. It is now maintained by a joint committee of the boroughs.

The Mansion, Gunnersbury Park, *c.* 1919. Gunnersbury Park Mansion, the larger of the two houses, now holds the local museum. Gunnersbury House is next to it behind the trees on the right and survives as the Small Mansion Arts Centre and flats.

London United Tram 334 on Uxbridge Road, Ealing, *c.* 1916. The tramlines were built with the help of Clifton Robinson after Ealing Council withdrew its objections to a tramway being built along Uxbridge Road. The first trams ran in 1901; as a result, shops opened along Uxbridge Road, a thriving shopping parade developed at West Ealing, and a housing estate opened at Northfields.

Uxbridge Road, West Ealing, *c.* 1907. This view shows the rows of shops built between Broughton Road and Drayton Green Road. It was among these parades that Jones and Knights opened a department store.

Uxbridge Road, West Ealing, *c.* 1907. Deans Park is on the right in this view, and the Cottage Hospital can just be seen at the far end of the road. It moved to Mattock Lane in 1911 and The Kinema Cinema was built on the site in 1913.

Uxbridge Road, West Ealing, *c.* 1907. Deans Park is on the left and the Primitive Methodist chapel is on the right on the corner with Bedford Road.

Left: Freeman, Hardy & Willis, 122 Uxbridge Road, Ealing, *c.* 1909. The shop was situated on the corner with Broughton Road, and Freeman Hardy & Willis still sell shoes from the premises today.

Below, left: No. 5 Woodville Road, Ealing, 1914. Ealing Tenants Ltd was formed in 1901 as a housing co-operative on the lines of that set up by Ebenezer Howard, who designed the garden cities of Letchworth (1902) and Welwyn (1919). The garden estate, called Brentham, was laid out from 1905 on fields near Pitshanger Park and the River Brent. *Below, right*: A small house in West Ealing, February 1911. The damage was caused by a storm which blew an elm tree on to the roof.

Uxbridge Road, West Ealing, *c.* 1909. Pitman's School is being advertised on the board. The pub sign of Ye Olde Hat stands on the corner of Talbot Road. The Old Hat pub is named on a map of 1777. A London United Tram has just passed.

Clark's College, Uxbridge Road, Ealing, 1910. There were branches of Pitman's, Clark's and Gregg's secretarial colleges in Ealing. On the boards outside, Civil Service courses are being advertised, some with exams to be taken in October 1910. An alleyway called Barnes Pikle was immediately to the left of Clark's College. The site was later used by the Young Women's Christian Association.

The Kinema, Northfields Avenue, *c.* 1913. Dean Gardens at Ealing Dean was an area of about 3 acres. When the Ealing Dean Cottage Hospital was moved to Mattock Lane in 1911, The Kinema Cinema was built on the site and opened in 1913. It was rebuilt as The Lido in 1928 and still bore this name in 1955. It later became an ABC cinema and, in 1997, a Belle-Vue cinema.

Shops on Northfield Avenue on the corner with Balfour Road, *c.* 1909. Northfields was an area promoted by publicity material produced by London United Trams when they arrived along the Uxbridge Road in 1901.

No. 72 Sydney Road, Northfields, *c.* 1913. Sydney Road was part of an estate in which the thoroughfares were named after places in Australia. Others included Adelaide Road, Brisbane Road, St Kilda Road and Melbourne Avenue. A library was built in 1903 on Melbourne Avenue, and the nave of St James' church was built in 1904 on St James' Avenue.

Northfields & Little Ealing station, Northfield Avenue, *c.* 1930. With a spacious and well-glazed booking hall, the station was opened on 11 December 1911 to replace the halt which had opened on the same site in 1908. The sign advertises the site of Northfields depot, built under the Development Act of 1929 for the relief of unemployment which was part of a 1930s back-to-work scheme. The chimney is part of Ealing District Steam Laundry.

Woodfield Road, Brentham, 1904. The earliest houses, which predate the Hampstead Garden Suburb, were nos 71 to 87 Woodfield Road, named Vivian Terrace after Henry Vivian MP, the prime mover in the enterprise. By 1905, fifty houses had been completed, which were stylistically ordinary small terraces.

Fowler's Walk, Brentham, *c.* 1910.

No. 43 Brunner Road, Brentham, 1910. In 1907 more land was bought and Raymond Unwin and Barry Parker, who had helped design the Hampstead Garden Suburb, were invited to lay out the estate. The other roads on the estate included Fowler's Walk, Denison Road, Neville Road, Brentham Way. The estate did not have as many social provisions as Hampstead but the Brentham Institute was opened in 1911 and St Barnabas' Church in 1916 .

Brentham Halt, January 1937. It was opened by the Great Western Railway in 1911 to serve the Brentham Garden estate. After Western Avenue opened, the area was settled by industry. Virol Foods Ltd, on the North Circular, can be seen in the background. Other companies in the area included the Kiwi Boot Polish Co., Arrow Electric, manufacturers of electrical switchgear, and S. Wolf & Co. Ltd, who produced portable electric tools. Amoco House stands in front of the former station, which closed in 1947 after Hanger Lane station opened.

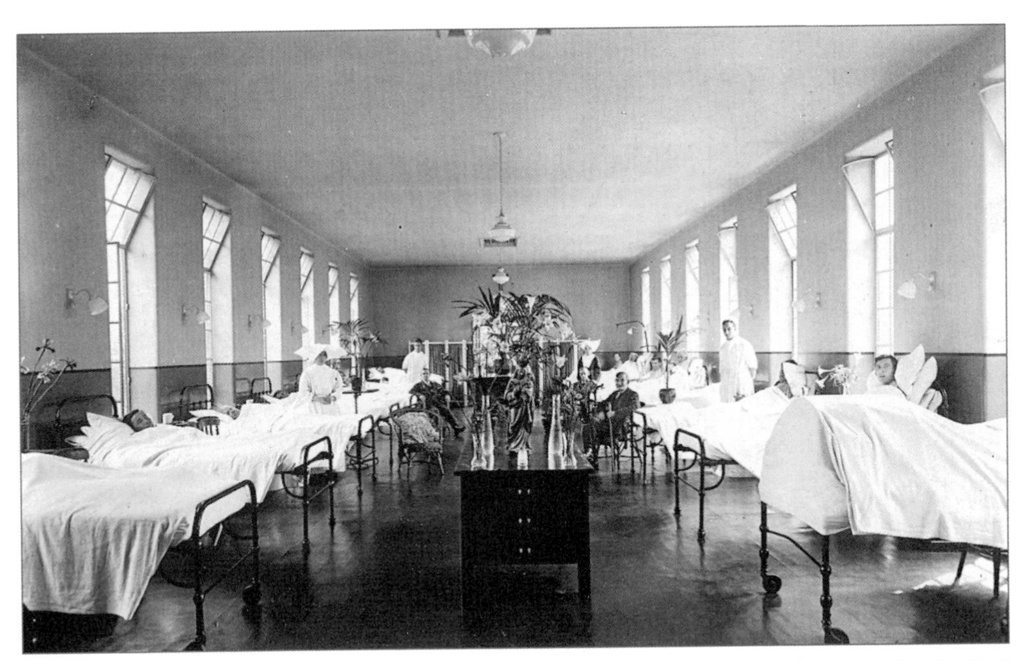

St Joseph's Ward, St David's Home, Castlebar Hill, Ealing, *c.* 1919. St David's Home for disabled ex-servicemen, situated in the middle of Castlebar Hill, was opened in 1918. It incorporates the remains of Henry de Bruno Austin's house on the site of Castle Hill Lodge and is still surrounded by large grounds. Having bought the Castle Hill Lodge estate from the Duke of Kent in 1860 to develop for housing, Austin went bankrupt in 1872. There is stained glass in the building designed in 1866 at the time of Austin's residence.

The Chapel, St David's Home, Castlebar Hill, Ealing, *c.* 1932. One of many additions, the chapel, added in 1919, was designed by A.S.G. Butler, in a classical rather than French style, with rusticated pilasters, a broken pediment and a central dome.

A first aid demonstration by Ealing Catholic School army cadet corps being inspected by some top brass in 1934. In 1916 Ealing Catholic School changed its name to Ealing Priory School when the church became a priory. In 1938 the school changed its name again becoming St Benet's, and in 1943 once again to St Benedict's.

Walpole Park, *c.* 1920. A large group of mostly women being addressed by a visiting dignitary in Walpole Park in the twenties.

Members of Ealing Cycle Club at a dinner in the twenties. Cycling was popular in the twenties when Middlesex was still a rural county.

The marriage of one of the Shellshears' children in the twenties. The Shellshears family opened an ironmonger's shop in 1902 at 94 Broadway, West Ealing. It was still there in 1930 but by 1955 it had moved to 154 Broadway.

Shellshears' advert of 1955.

Ealing Broadway, *c*. 1929. The J. Sainsbury & Co. motor van is just delivering to the Ealing store on the right. The twenties and thirties saw the rise of the multiples like Sainsburys, Boots, Woolworths, Marks and Spencer and W.H. Smith. Sainsburys started with one shop in Kentish Town in 1873 and by 1939 had expanded to 250 branches. The building on the right was built in 1883.

A motor delivery van of Eldred Sayers & Son, Ealing, *c*. 1928. The crest of the Metropolitan Borough of Ealing can be seen above the head of the white-coated driver. Eldred Sayers & Son was a department store on Ealing Broadway.

New Broadway, Uxbridge Road, Ealing, 1932. The tram is a Feltham tram car, which operated on London United's service 7 from 5 January 1931 to 15 November 1936 when it was replaced by trolleybuses. Car Mart Ltd and Electronic House have been demolished. Offices were built on the site between 1980 and 1983 and the council has occupied it as the Civic Centre from 1987.

The Broadway stations, *c.* 1931. On the right is the Great Western Railway pagoda-style station, which was rebuilt as an office block in 1965. The Underground Railway's station is further down on the right with the bus outside it. A General no. 97A bus running between Ealing and Northfields has just pulled in.

Gunnersbury Avenue Estate

EALING

Tudor Way and Carbery Avenue

Only a few plots on this very popular Estate are now left, and if a house of distinction in the Tudor style appeals to you, come along without further delay.

The Estate is only 4 minutes walk from Acton Town Station, District Railway, and under the improved service, 20 minutes from Piccadilly Circus.

Prices—With 4 Bedrooms, from **£1,850** Freehold

Full particulars can be obtained from

A. LYFORD,

WEST LODGE, ACTON, W. 3

'Phone: ACORN 2426

or at the office on the Estate at the corner of Tudor Way

'Phone: ACORN 0433

An estate agent's advert for Gunnersbury Avenue in 1933.

No. 27, Hillsboro, *c.* 1930. This large semi-detached house in Ealing is part of one of the many estates constructed in the 1930s. These included Gunnersbury Avenue, Hanger Hill and the Greystoke estate on Western Avenue.

W. Smart's Fowler No. 14877 *Little Margaret*, fitted with a car-lifting crane, busy constructing fairground rides on Ealing Common, 8 June 1943.

New Broadway, Ealing, *c.* 1950, with a 607 trolleybus stopping at the beacon crossing next to the underground toilets, which are no longer there. On the right scaffolding surrounds Christ Church, which had been bombed during the war. It was rebuilt between 1946 and 1952, and renamed Christ the Saviour. It incorporated the parish of St Saviour, whose church was also bombed but not rebuilt.

ABERNETHIE

and Son Ltd.

Official Outfitters
to
St. Anne's School

★ This is just to remind you that ABERNETHIE & SON LTD. are Specialists, not only for the Regulation School Uniform, but also Girls' Clothes for Holidays and all occasions.

143-5 UXBRIDGE ROAD, WEST EALING
W.13

Telephone - - - Ealing 5114 & 5115

An advert of 1950 for Abernethie and Son Ltd, who provided uniforms for other schools in the area as well as St Anne's, which was attended by the author's mother.

The author's mother in her garden at Ealing Park Gardens in 1954. The dress she is wearing is blue and the cat she is stroking was called Monty. Bill Carrol, a next-door neighbour, is leaning over the fence. He was gassed during the First World War and he built the shed he is standing next to.

The Golf Links, Perivale Lane, Perivale, seen here in *c.* 1951, are part of Ealing Golf Club, which opened in 1898 with an eighteen-hole golf course. Before that, in 1894, there was a rifle range on the site, which was used by the Ealing Rifle Volunteers, forerunners of the Territorial Army.

Perivale bowling green, *c.* 1951. The bowling green and pavilion are still in situ at the end of Bellvue Road, Ealing. Perivale bowling club used to play on this green next to Pitshanger bowling club, until the former moved to Alperton Lane, Alperton. Pitshanger is now the only bowling club based here. Ealing and the British Legion bowling club play at Perivale Park.

South Ealing Road, South Ealing, *c.* 1961. Manley Motors is on the left, opposite is H.A. Roberts on the corner with Durham Road. A Vauxhall Velox is on the right, cut by the edge of the photograph, and behind the van is an Austin A40. Partly visible on the left is a Thames van and further up on the left is the photographer's car, a Standard Ensign.

Ealing Broadway, *c.* 1961. The Ealing Hippodrome, which housed the Palladium Cinema from 1914 to 1958, has been demolished and replaced by W.H. Smith on the right. The spire of Christ the Saviour overlooks the Broadway. A Ford van is on the left and a Messerschmidt bubble car is waiting at the traffic lights with an Express Dairies milk float and a Lyons van parked behind.

A bus on route 112 on Uxbridge Road, Ealing Common, on 30 April 1967. Many of the bodies for these buses were made nearby at Park Royal. Although this bus is not a Routemaster there is a Routemaster Heritage Centre at Trumper's Way, Hanwell.

A bus on route 65A in Argyle Road, Ealing, on 16 November 1968. Its destination was the Copt Gilders estate near Chessington.

SECTION TWO

HANWELL

The Lock, Hanwell, *c.* 1900. The building of the Grand Union Canal in 1794 straightened the course of the Brent. At Hanwell the Grand Union Canal rises from the valley of the Brent by a flight of six locks and a further two at Norwood. The lowest of the six locks is seen here near the asylum at Hanwell.

The name 'Hanwell' probably means cock-frequented stream, from the old English 'hana', a cock, and 'wielle' meaning a stream or spring. Hanwell was given to Westminster Abbey by King Edgar in 959. Hanwell, Greenford, Perivale and Northolt were in Elthorne, one of the six hundreds of Middlesex. A hundred was a district capable of supporting a hundred groups of ten settlers. This explains why the name Elthorne is common in Hanwell with Elthorne Park, Elthorne Park Road, Elthorne Avenue, Elthorne Heights, and Hanwell and Elthorne station temporarily using the name too. The medieval village grew around St Mary's Church. In 1838 the Great Western Railway opened a station at Hanwell. In the mid-nineteenth century Hanwell was famous for its large institutions, including the Central London District School, the County Lunatic Asylum housing 2,500 patients, and two cemeteries, the combined presence of which discouraged Victorian expansion in the area. Its image improved after the local board supported a route for trams along Uxbridge Road. Businesses opened along Uxbridge Road and the tram depot was even built on it. In the twenties and thirties a new estate was built on Boston Road, served by a rebuilt Boston Manor station on the Piccadilly Line. By this time, in1926, Hanwell had already merged with Ealing.

St Mary's Church, Hanwell, seen here in *c.* 1905, was built on the site of a twelfth-century church. It was designed in 1841 by Gilbert Scott, who designed Christ Church, Ealing, in 1852. Here at Hanwell, flint was preferred to Kentish ragstone. Dedications to St Mary were popular in this area, and can also be found at Perivale, Twyford, Northolt Green, South Ealing, Acton and Norwood.

Churchfield's recreation ground, *c.* 1928. The 22-acre site was bought in 1898.

Wharnecliffe Viaduct at Hanwell, *c.* 1913. The bridge was Isambard Kingdom Brunel's first major structure, and was built in 1835–8 to carry the Great Western Railway line over the River Brent. Brunel copied the elliptical form used for other bridges, including the one at Maidenhead over the Thames. The station was opened in June 1838. It was rebuilt in 1875–7, when the viaduct too was renovated, being doubled in width in 1877. The station was called Hanwell in 1876, and had been renamed Hanwell and Elthorne station by 1936.

Wharnecliffe Viaduct, *c.* 1900. The eight elliptical arches each have a 21-metre span and are 5.3 metres high, resting on brick piers in the Egyptian style. In the centre are the arms of Lord Wharnecliffe, the Chairman of the Parliamentary Committee, which examined the building of this railway, including the viaduct. Wharnecliffe bat caves, named after the Chairman, are situated in the Brent River Park, which was created by Ealing in the 1970s after proposals by the Brent River and Canal Society.

Conolly Dell, *c.* 1905. Dr John Conolly was the superintendent of the Middlesex County Lunatic Asylum at Hanwell from 1839, and was famous for introducing techniques of non-restraint to asylums. Conolly Dell was part of the grounds of The Lawn, now Station Road, where Dr Conolly lived after his retirement. He died in 1866.

St George's Cemetery, Uxbridge Road, Hanwell, *c.* 1906. The City of Westminster cemetery was designed by Robert Jerrard, with a large lodge, Gothic gatepiers and an avenue of cedars leading to the chapels. It opened in 1854. The Kensington cemetery, designed by Thomas Allom, was built opposite in 1855.

The Central London District School for the poor, or the Cuckoo Schools, *c*. 1909. It was built between 1856 and 1857 in the grounds of Hanwell Park, by Tress and Chambers, to cater for over 1,000 Poor Law pupils. After the school closed in 1933 the land was sold for housing development (1933–9) as part of the London County Council Cuckoo estate. The administrative block was reused and is now the Hanwell Community Centre in Westcott Crescent.

Central London District School sports team, Hanwell, 1909. Winners of the Whitehall, Portsmouth and London Shields, junior boys cup and junior girls cup. Charlie Chaplin spent two years, from the age of seven to nine (1896–8), at the Central London District School for the poor. In 1996 a plaque commemorating this star of the silver screen was put up on the former school by the 100 Years of Cinema organization, in association with the British Film Institute, to mark the centenary of the cinema.

Our Lady and St Joseph Roman Catholic Church, Hanwell, *c.* 1901. In 1854 Miss Ann Rabnett invited the Roman Catholic mission at Turnham Green to serve mass in a room at her home, Clifden Lodge, St George's Road, Hanwell. When this became too small she gave land next to Clifden Lodge for a chapel dedicated to St Augustine, which stood on the site of today's church. Later the chapel was served by a priest from the Pious Society of the Missions at Saffron Hill until the church above was opened in 1864 and a priest was appointed. It was designed by Pugin but was not consecrated until 1918 because it was not free of debt until then. It was replaced with the present modern building in 1967.

Baptist and Congregational Union Free Church, Westminster Road, Hanwell, *c.* 1907. The church was opened on this site in 1869, and in 1870 the schoolroom was built alongside. Both of these were extended in 1878. The pastor in the 1920s was Donald E. Sutton. In 1952 the church severed its Congregational connection and became purely Baptist. The main church building has been demolished and the site is now part of the forecourt of the Warwick Wright Peugeot dealership. The school building behind is still there and is now used by The Apostolic Catholic Assyrian Church of the East.

St Mark's Church and school hall, Lower Boston Road, Hanwell, *c.* 1902. St Mark's Church schools were established on this site in 1855 with many extensions (in 1871, 1884, 1895). A tall cruciform plan building with an apsed chancel, St Mark's Church was built in 1879 by William White. The nave was completed in 1883 but the intended tower and spire were not built. The church was converted to flats in 1989 and has been renamed St Mark's Court.

Hanwell fire engine, Hanwell Broadway, 1896. There was also a fire brigade at Hanwell Asylum. Hanwell Broadway still looks very rural in the days before the trams and commercial businesses arrived along Uxbridge Road.

HANWELL PARK

Hanwell Park Mansion was a Georgian house, standing in its own parkland, owned by the Millett family in the sixteenth and seventeenth centuries. By the eighteenth century West Middlesex had become a fashionable neighbourhood, secluded yet convenient for London. Hanwell Park was for a time the residence of Sir Archibald Macdonald, Chief Baron of the Exchequer in the reign of George III and known as the 'Knight of a thousand and one tales' for his fame as a raconteur. Benjamin Sharpe bought the house in 1848 and sold the north-east part of the park in 1857 as a site for the Central London District School. After his death in 1883 the mansion and lands passed to his son Sir Montague Sharpe, well known for his work on the history of Middlesex and for his theory of Caesar's crossing of the Thames at Brentford.

Sir Montague sold Hanwell Park in 1884 and the south-east part of the estate was developed with new houses on Framfield, Cowper, Milton and Shakespeare Roads between 1894 and 1914. The house was bought in 1897 by J.C. Johnstone and survived until 1913 when it was demolished and Drayton Manor Secondary School was built on the site. The remaining north-west corner towards Greenford and the River Brent, known as Elthorne Heights, was built over with private housing by 1935. In 1936 81 acres in the south-west corner were reserved for Brent Valley Golf Course. When the Central London District School closed in 1933 the north-east part of the estate was again developed, with 1,592 houses completed by 1939. The administrative buildings of the school were retained and the tree-lined drive that led to the school was preserved in the road layout as Cuckoo Avenue.

Hanwell Park Mansion, *c.* 1840.

The entrance gates to The Grove, with the adjacent lodge, Cuckoo Lane, *c.* 1923. The Grove was a house built in the late eighteenth century.

Manor Court Road, *c.* 1923. Manor Court Road, Golden Manor and Manor House School are all modern names. None of them has any connection with an ancient manor. Manor Court Road was laid out by 1894, when the first houses were built.

Park Hotel, Hanwell, *c.* 1905. The 'Park' of the hotel's name comes from Hanwell Park. Part of the building was used as a theatre and cinema. Known as the Park Theatre, it was also used by the Questors amateur dramatic group until 1923. It was still a theatre in 1955. The theatre has now been demolished and recently replaced by flats called Kipling Court, which perpetuates the famous poets theme, after whom many of the surrounding roads are named.

Church Road and Greenford Avenue, Hanwell, *c.* 1905. The Park Hotel, which contained the Park Theatre, is on the far right of Greenford Avenue. Church Road, forking to the left, leads to Hanwell station. The building in the centre of the picture is Victoria Mansions.

Greenford Avenue, Hanwell, 1912. The former Cuckoo Lane provided access to the Hanwell Park and Hanwell Grove estates. The parade of shops on the right is between Milton Road and Shakespeare Road. The shops served the new residents on both the Hanwell Park and Hanwell Grove estates.

Greenford Avenue, Hanwell, *c*. 1912. The shops on the right are between Drayton Bridge Road and Framfield Road.

Grove Avenue, seen here in *c.* 1912, was named after the Hanwell Grove estate on which it was built in 1897. Grove Avenue was built on land to the east of the original Hanwell Park Mansion.

Shakespeare Road, *c.* 1913. Laid out in 1894 at the same time as Framfield Road, this was part of the Hanwell Park estate, built on the south-east part of the former Hanwell Park. The roads were named after famous poets, and included Milton Road, Cowper Road, Dryden Avenue and Browning Avenue.

Milton Road, *c.* 1912. The right-hand side of the road has not been developed for housing yet. On 27 August 1885 a Local Board was established for the government of Hanwell but under the provisions of the Local Government Act 1894 an Urban District Council was established in its place. It was this organization which helped in the development of new estates at Hanwell Grove and Hanwell Park.

Cowper Road, *c.* 1912. The road was named after William Cowper (1731–1800), the English poet who wrote *The Diverting History of John Gilpin* and *The Task* in 1785.

The inauguration of electric tram services with a procession passing The Parade, Uxbridge Road, Hanwell, 10 July 1901. The electric trams reduced operating costs and allowed reduced fares for the working classes. Ealing objected to the trams because of their working-class associations but Hanwell's support ensured their adoption.

WXF Blake, Electric Joinery Works, Hanwell, *c.* 1910. Electricity was replacing gas at this time and the tramway companies like London United were often the electricity suppliers because they ran the tramway with their own generators. It is not surprising to see this electricity joinery works at Hanwell, where there was already a tram depot.

Brent Bridge, Uxbridge Road, Hanwell, *c.* 1902. This road bridge across the Brent valley had a nineteenth-century balustraded stone parapet. On the west side the three eighteenth-century brick arches are said to incorporate two arches from a medieval bridge.

The new Brent Bridge, Uxbridge Road, Hanwell, was rebuilt between 1905 and 1906 to allow the trams to pass over it more easily, and is seen here after its completion. The County of London pauper lunatic asylum is in the background behind the bridge. One of the tram stops was known as the Asylum Gates.

Seward Road, Hanwell, *c.* 1913. The arrival of the trams in 1901 helped to increase Hanwell's population from 10,438 in 1901 to 19,129 in 1911, an increase of 83 per cent. From 1894, estates were built at Hanwell Park and Hanwell Grove to the north of Uxbridge Road. South of Uxbridge Road, estates were built off Boston Road and around St George's cemetery at Seward Road and Deans Road.

Deans Road, Hanwell, seen here in *c.* 1932, is named after Mr Dean, who owned the field over which the road was built.

Vaux's Corner, Hanwell. Vaux was a draper in 1913, who had founded his business on this corner in 1819. The trams arrived in 1901. The old parish church and village centre was around St Mary's near the River Brent but the trams helped the business centre to move along the Uxbridge Road.

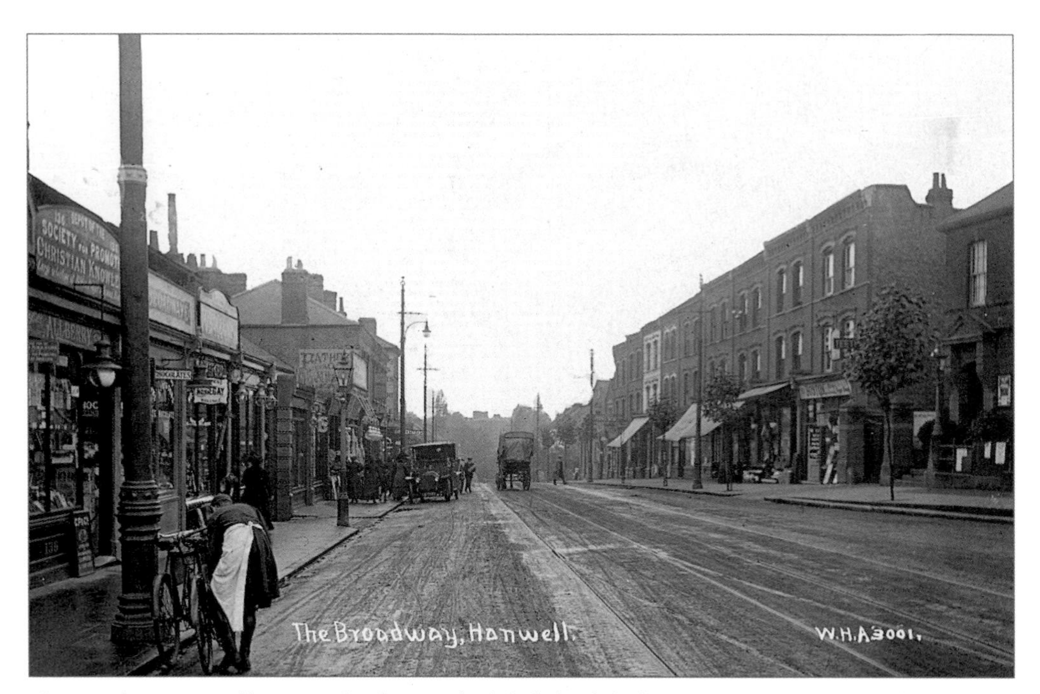

The Broadway, Hanwell, 1914. The shop on the left, behind the lamp post, is no. 136, the depot for the Society for the Promotion of Christian Knowledge (SPCK). The shops further down on the left have been demolished and the area is now the forecourt of a car dealership. In the middle of the picture in the distance is the London County Asylum. The local police station is in the right foreground.

The Parade, Uxbridge Road, Hanwell, 1910. The arrival of the trams in 1901 increased Hanwell's population and new shops were built to serve this growing population. The Coronation Picture Palace was built on Uxbridge Road to entertain the new residents, but it did not last long.

The Parade, Uxbridge Road, Hanwell, 1905. The Parade was one of the shopping parades that was built on the Broadway, Hanwell, to take advantage of the passing trade on the trams between Ealing and Uxbridge. The shop with the white face, on the right, is Longman's shop, shown opposite.

Longman's the outfitters, 121 Uxbridge Road, Hanwell, *c.* 1902. By 1930 it belonged to Mrs Clara Scrutton, a costumier.

St Ann's School, Springfield Road, was opened in 1902. A good example of the Board School period (1870–1902), this school is still there today. Forster's Education Act of 1870 enabled local authorities to set up school boards who could impose a school rate and acquire land on which to build new board schools if there were not enough places in existing schools for all the children in the District. In 1902 Balfour's Education Act abolished school boards and replaced them with local education authorities.

Hanwell Wesleyan football team, *c.* 1906. Methodism had a large working-class following and football was very much a working-class sport. Hanwell Town Football Club played at Elthorne Park in the thirties and now play at Perivale. Brentford were in the First Division from 1935 to 1947.

The Wesleyan church, Church Road, Hanwell, *c.* 1906.

The Wesleyan church, Church Road, Hanwell, *c.* 1911. The building was designed by Gordon and Gunton and opened in 1904. Wesleyan Methodists, a group which was formed in the eighteenth century, became United Methodists in 1907 and part of the Methodist Church in 1932. The Wesleyan church became Hanwell Methodist church in 1932 and it is still there today, with Hanwell Health Centre to the left and flats to the right. The railings on the left belong to the church of St Mellitus with St Mark, built on Church Road by A. Blomfield between 1909 and 1910.

Park Road, Hanwell, 1920. Park Road took its name from Hanwell Park. The Wesleyan church and St Mellitus with St Mark were well placed to serve the new residents of the Hanwell Park estate.

Cherington Road, Hanwell, *c.* 1905. The white house in the left corner, belonging to L.N. Wiles, builder's and decorator's, is currently a private house and the building next to it, advertising E. Howell, Coal & Coke, is now occupied by Mizler Wright & Co., solicitors. The road was known as Church Road in 1896, but was renamed. The Local Board bought Cherington House as a meeting place in 1891.

A church procession on Cherington Road, Hanwell, 19 September 1909. In 1905 the public library, or Carnegie Library, was built in Cherington Road by Hanwell Urban District Council, to which Andrew Carnegie donated £3,000. He also donated to the Andrew Carnegie Library at Brentford in 1903. The Grand Theatre (later the Curzon) on Cherington Road was open by 1917 but closed in 1955.

A meeting held in Hanwell during the First World War. The flags of the Triple Entente (France, Great Britain, Russia) are hanging around the walls. The men in the picture look as if they are wearing the blue uniforms of convalescents. Many ladies from the Borough of Ealing worked as nurses in the military hospitals, particularly in Southall. Men from the Ealing Borough formed the Senior Voluntary Aid Detachment (VAD) in the county and received the wounded at the VAD Hospital in Southall, among others. They also worked as Special Constables and for the Royal Army Medical Corps.

Hanwell Salvation Army Band, *c.* 1925. The bandmaster was K. Eacott.

Hanwell Salvation Army Band, West London Division, 1927. In 1930 Lt.-Col. Charles Bax was the Divisional Commander, and the Divisional HQ was at 14 Broadway, West Ealing. The Salvation Army was founded by William Booth as the 'Christian Mission' in East London in 1865. It first took the name Salvation Army in 1878. In that year the first brass band featured at an Army event, and led to their formation in other groups. In 1880 standard uniforms were adopted. During the First World War it was active as an agency of goodwill and compassion, which helped to gain it acceptance. It is active today in 74 countries with 2 million members.

E.E. Nicholass, the butcher, Uxbridge Road, Hanwell, *c.* 1929.

Church Road bridge was rebuilt and widened by the Great Western Railway during May 1925 to allow greater access to the new estates along Greenford Avenue. The original bridge was known as Haffenden's Bridge, after a local family. The new bridge was built by lowering it on top of the old bridge with steam cranes, and then demolishing the old bridge underneath. Although the bridge looks in a state of disrepair, with the original bridge still visible below the girder, a Great Western engine with a passenger train is already crossing it.

A Super Sentinel steamwagon of Charles Kirby, Cambridge Road, Hanwell, *c.* 1925. During the first half of the twentieth century the number of small factories and workshops in the area increased greatly: many of them lay south of the Uxbridge Road, between St Margaret's Road and Cambridge Road. Cambridge Yard was first used industrially in 1919 and the letting of workshops started in 1924.

A Model T Ford motor delivery van of the Fresh Air Hand Laundry, Hanwell, *c.*1923. The proprietress was Mrs Davis.

Hanwell London United Tramways (LUT) depot on Uxbridge Road during May 1927, before it was rebuilt. Tram no. 308 is on route 7A to Shepherd's Bush and the one behind has a headboard for Brentford.

Hanwell LUT depot, Uxbridge Road, Hanwell, *c.* 1929. The depot is on the left, behind the tram. The Kings Arms, on the right, was rebuilt in 1930. Also on the right is Boston Farm Dairy, distributing through Long and Pocock.

Hanwell depot being rebuilt for trolleybuses during October 1936. The new depot opened on 15 November 1936 with capacity for 108 trolleybuses. These operated on route 607 and 655. Route 607 operated between Shepherd's Bush and Uxbridge, and replaced tram route 7. It was the busiest single trolleybus service and operated only out of Hanwell depot.

Hanwell Trolleybus depot, May 1937. When the depot closed on 8 November 1960, the trolleybuses were replaced by buses. On a site opposite St Bernard's Hospital gates, Southall Bus Garage had already been built ready for the buses as early as 1933. The trolleybus depot has recently been demolished and is an open space awaiting development. Hanwell's transport links are still celebrated today by the Routemaster Heritage Centre at Trumper's Way, Hanwell.

The Parade, Uxbridge Road, Hanwell, *c.* 1937. Wakefield's photographer's shop, no. 84, is seen in the picture. They took this photograph and many others of Ealing. The Parade was situated between St George's Road and Boston Road, and included George Stacey's, wardrobe dealer, Tom Smith's, J.T. Ingleton's, Hanwell Herbalist Stores, Broadway Shoe Stores, Wakefield's, and Barnikel's Garage.

Uxbridge Road, Hanwell, *c.* 1930. This parade is between Boston Road and George Street. It includes E.S. Gould's, a butcher and poulterer, Muirhead's Library at no.136, which has replaced the depot of the SPCK (see p. 64), F. Gwyther's, a confectioner, W. Platford's, a wholesale tobacconist, and W. Southwood's, a bootmaker. Daren Bread, a baker's, is on the other side of George Street. Today, no. 136 survives but some of the shops have been demolished and the area is part of a garage forecourt.

Hanwell Broadway, 1937. The row of shops and businesses is, from left to right, the Duke of York pub, William Parsons', a watchmaker, Ripon's and Barclays Bank. Traffic lights have been set up and a 1930s clock has been built outside the bank. Trolleybus wires are in place and the tramlines have gone.

Hanwell Broadway, 1937. Cole's, the builders' merchants, and the post office were built in the thirties next to the Vaux building.

CUCKOO ESTATE,

Greenford Avenue, Hanwell, W. 7

Perspective View of Block of Four Houses.

£5 Deposit secures. Small Deposit. Balance as rent.
Low Repayments from about **28s. 6d.** per week (including Rates).
NO Road or Legal Charges. ROOM FOR GARAGE.
Always open for Inspection.

These attractive well-built houses are conveniently situated in the best residential part of Hanwell, in the Borough of Ealing.
There is a bus service to Hanwell Station, and also services to Ealing Broadway (G.W. Central London and District) Stations.
There are good shopping facillties in Greenford Avenue, and Schools are also close.

£750 Freehold

No visitors to the above Estate can fail to be impressed at the splendid value offered by Messrs. Tucker & Warren with their charming Tudor-type houses, the main features of the houses are the sound footings, concrete over-site, and well timbered roofs.

For the lady of the house, the all-tiled Kitchen, with independent boiler, roomy larder fitted with tiled cold slab, is a very pleasing feature—greatly appreciated.

There are two Reception Rooms, three Bedrooms, separate Lavatory and Bathroom, with airing cupboard to latter.

A Glass Verandah overlooks the garden—an asset to any houses with casement doors, and cement path to all gardens with close-boarded fence all round.

For full particulars apply to the Builders—

TUCKER & WARREN,

21, Hill View Villas, Greenford Avenue, Hanwell, W.7
Tel.: PERIVALE 1696 **(or on the site).**

or to

RAYMOND J. WARD, F.S.I., Architect & Chartered Surveyor,
107, Uxbridge Road, Ealing, W.5. **(Tel.: Ealing 5650).**

Estate Office open daily and week ends, Sun. incl., from 9 a.m. till dusk.

An estate agent's advert for houses on Cuckoo Avenue, Hanwell, 1933. The population of Hanwell had increased from 19,129 in 1911 to 20,485 in 1921. In 1926 Hanwell was included in the Corporation of Ealing.

A single-deck tram car on Boston Road, Hanwell, opposite Boston Dining Rooms near the corner with Jessamine Road, 1926. The Brentford to Hanwell via Boston Road route opened on 26 May 1906. The London United Tram service 55 had operated between Hanwell and Brentford along Boston Road and was replaced by trolleybus route 655 on 13 December 1936. This operated on a circular route between Hammersmith, Brentford and Acton and was eventually extended to Clapham Junction in 1937.

No. 184 Boston Road, *c.* 1930. House building had continued in the twenties along Boston Road, which had been widened for the trams. No. 184 was next door to St Thomas's Church, which was rebuilt in 1933 (see p. 83). Likewise, Boston Manor station was rebuilt in 1934, improving facilities for the many new residents.

ST THOMAS'S CHURCH, BOSTON ROAD

In 1929 St Thomas's was still an iron mission church seating 300 people. In 1933 the church was taken over by the London Diocesan Home Mission, which had been patron of St Thomas's Church, Portman Square. St Thomas's, Boston Road, was paid for from the proceeds of the sale of St Thomas's, Portman Square. The new church cost £14,225 and was designed to seat 428 people. The parish assigned to it in 1933 consisted of part of St Mellitus's parish, which in turn had been detached from St Mary's, Hanwell. The foundation stone was laid on 8 July 1933 by the Earl of Jersey.

St Thomas's was designed by Sir Edward Maufe in 1933. It is important both as the forerunner to Maufe's Guildford Cathedral and for its contemporary sculpture and furnishings representing the best efforts of English religious art of the 1930s. At St Thomas's, the plain and high central nave contrasts with two intimate low side chapels. The exterior is of brown brick with paler bands, but inside the concrete is exposed in the walls and the plain unribbed cross-vaults.

The religious art is found both inside and out at St Thomas's. The street runs along the east side, which displays a crucifixion by Eric Gill against and below a round east window beside a tall, square, north-east tower with a green copper cap. All the other windows are narrow lancets, the largest one at the centre of the west side. Over the north door there are doves carved by Vernon Hill. Fittings include wall panels by Moira Forsyth, one of which is entitled 'Suffer Little Children', and depicted in the pale colours of the Arts and Craft movement. There are also two limed oak organ screens and a stone Virgin and Child in the Lady Chapel, all by the sculptor Vernon Hill.

St Thomas's Church, Boston Road, Hanwell, 1934.

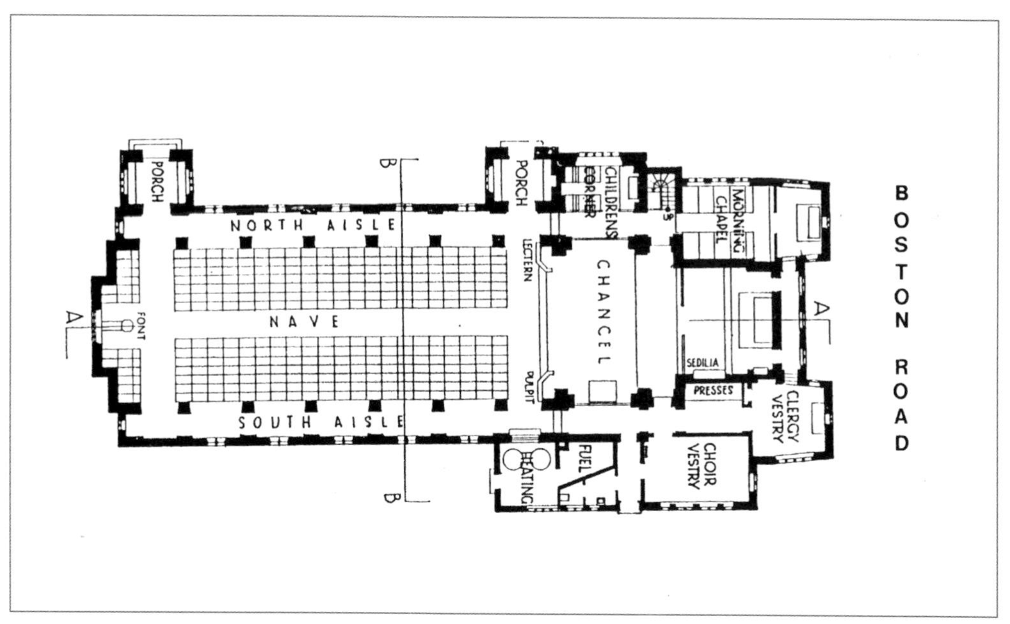

The plan of St Thomas's, Boston Road, 1933.

Guildford Cathedral; the similarities in design between St Thomas's Church, Hanwell, and the cathedral are evident in this drawing. The minimal Gothic style is echoed, with a brown-brick exterior disguising a concrete interior, a long central nave with chapels and side rooms off the chancel (see plan above), lancet windows and tiny clerestory windows. Maufe used Vernon Hill at Guildford too, for the three-seated sedilia of Doulting stone with smiling angels.

Sheep grazing on the Brent Valley Golf Links, Hanwell, near St Mary's, *c.* 1936. Brent Valley Golf Course was registered in 1936 with 81 acres. Land east of the River Brent in Hanwell was registered in 1937 with 4.25 acres.

A London Transport bus on Greenford Avenue, near Hall Drive, Hanwell, 1955. The council estate has been built on the site of the Cuckoo Schools. Route 55 went from Greenford to Brentford via Northfields.

SECTION THREE

GREENFORD INCLUDING PERIVALE, TWYFORD & NORTHOLT

King Edward VII and Queen Alexandra passing Ravenor Park estate, 1912. The first road to be laid out was Ravenor Park Road, which is seen here.

Grenan forda is first mentioned in 845, in a legal transaction. In the seventeenth century, as urbanization began to spread, development in the Greenford area was dominated by two families, the Costons and the Ravenors. An Urban District Council of nine members was formed in 1894 for Greenford, Perivale and Twyford and the district was divided into four wards: Greenford, Greenford Green, Perivale and Twyford Abbey. The population of Greenford at this time was growing: from 545 in 1891 to 672 in 1901. In 1904 the Great Western Railway reached Greenford from Old Oak and a branch opened to Greenford from Ealing. Building on Ravenor Park estate, the first housing estate in Greenford, was begun in 1912 and included Ravenor Park Road. In 1924 Greenford Road was built, replacing Oldfield Lane as the main north–south route. In 1926 the Urban District was merged with the Metropolitan Borough of Ealing. Western Avenue cut across the area in 1934 and house building filled in the areas between these major trunk roads; by 1940 the whole area was built up.

Greenford Green, *c.* 1900, at the junction of Oldfield Lane and Horsenden Lane, showing the oldest post-box in England which was placed there in 1856. Greenford Green is where the chemical works of William Henry Perkin and Sons opened in 1856 and first produced aniline dyes, which completely altered the process of dyeing in the cotton, woollen and silk trades. The works closed in 1885 and by 1908 the buildings had been taken over by a firm of bone boilers; by 1935 a tallow factory had been set up in them. Greenford Green Farm, with its seventeenth-century barn, was still there in 1933. The sign at Sudbury Hill station read 'Sudbury Hill station for Greenford Green'.

A row of cottages on Oldfield Lane, Greenford Green, next to the bridge over the Grand Union Canal, *c.* 1913. Today the cottages have been demolished and the Glaxo Factory (opened in 1935) extends behind the cottages on the other side of the canal. There was a canal wharf at Greenford Green which encouraged the siting of factories near this transport system in the days before Greenford Road and Western Avenue were built.

Manor Farm, Greenford, 1912. The farm adjoined the Ravenor Park estate and Holy Cross Church. In 1894 the farmer was Thomas Smith Job. Other farms in Greenford included Greenford Farm, Coston's Farm, Stanhope Park Farm, Greenford Green Farm and Ravenor Farm. Manor Farm was still there in 1936, but now East Close and Henley Close off Ferrymead Gardens have been built on the site.

The top of the hill at Oldfield Lane, Greenford, 1912. The building on the right is the stable building of Stanhope Park, the home of Mr Edward Otter, who was Sheriff of Middlesex in 1909–10. In the distance the roof of Costons House can just be seen, which was next to the Ravenor Park estate. Stanhope Park Road had been built on Stanhope Park estate by 1936.

The foundation stone laying ceremony for the first house on the Ravenor Park estate on 22 April 1912. Ravenor is a name long associated with Greenford; in the seventeenth century Symo Ravenor was Constable of Greenford and a member of the jury of a court held in 1638. Today Ravenor Park Recreation Ground, which was open by 1936, preserves the Ravenor name.

Costons Lane, opposite the Ravenor Park estate, 1912. Costons Lane was named after Simon Coston, a foundling who disappeared from the village and returned a rich man. He died in 1637. The name was also preserved by Costons House and Farm (now demolished but still there in 1936), Costons Avenue and Costons School (built 1937). In Greenford church there are five marble floor slabs and some brasses, including one to the Coston family dated 1637, which includes the names of Simon Coston's father, his wife Bridget, a baby boy and five daughters. The Costons gave a font to both Greenford and Perivale churches.

Ravenor House on Oldfield Lane is on the left, next to the gate at the entrance to a footpath, in this photograph taken in 1912. The entrance to the Ravenor Park estate can be seen on the right in the distance. This is now Ravenor Park Road, leading to Greenford Gardens. Ravenor House was still in situ in 1936 but has since been demolished.

The road from Greenford village (Oldfield Lane) to the Ravenor Park estate, Great Greenford. The athletes about to climb the hill are in the London Business Houses Walking Championship on 11 May 1912, from Greenford Green to Northolt, which was won by E.C. Brown. On the right a board advertises freehold plots with £5 down at the entrance to the estate. Further on the right, in front of Costons House, is a board advertising a block of shops.

The old post office, Oldfield Lane, Greenford village, *c.* 1915. J. Raven was a grocer who ran the village store and post office. On the other side of the village green was L.C. Hatch the butcher. Sainsburys now occupies the site of J. Raven.

Greenford war memorial in Greenford village was unveiled on 12 June 1921 by Mr C. Fane de Salis, Chairman of the Middlesex County Council. Mr and Mrs A.W. Perkin, who owned the chemical factory, were also at the ceremony. The memorial was designed by Councillor A.J. Campbell Cooper; its inscription reads: 'Ye who live on mid English pastures green, remember us and think what might have been'. On the left are the cottages which, in 1912, included a butcher's, and on the right is a row of cottages including the post office and J. Raven's, the grocer.

Oldfield Lane, Greenford, 1937. In 1869 a mission worker sent to Greenford to help the poor found no drainage or water supply, no street lights or transport, and consequently a low life expectancy. In 1925 Greenford was still a rural area, with numerous farms, a blacksmith's shop and wheelwright's, and cows herded through the country lanes.

Greenford schoolhouse, Oldfield Lane, 1935. It was built in 1878 by the Revd Edward Betham of Holy Cross, Greenford, who also rebuilt the chancel of Holy Cross in 1871. In 1939 Sir Albert Richardson's New Holy Cross Church, Greenford, was built.

Costons Lane, Greenford, *c.* 1925. The lane was split by the Greenford Road, which was built in 1924. This view shows nos 108 to 90, on the left side of Costons Lane. The tree on the right has now gone. Costons Parade was built around the corner and the Coston name is also celebrated by nearby Costons Avenue. Route 97 was extended to Greenford station in 1928. Jubilee Parade was built on Greenford Road in 1935, and Maltman's Parade too at a later date.

Frederick G. Skinner's confectioner's shop, Oldfield Lane, Greenford, *c.* 1930. The shop was on the corner of Ravenor Park Road and Oldfield Lane.

See GOODHEW'S DELIGHTFUL HOUSES on the

STANHOPE ESTATE,

Ruislip Road, GREENFORD.

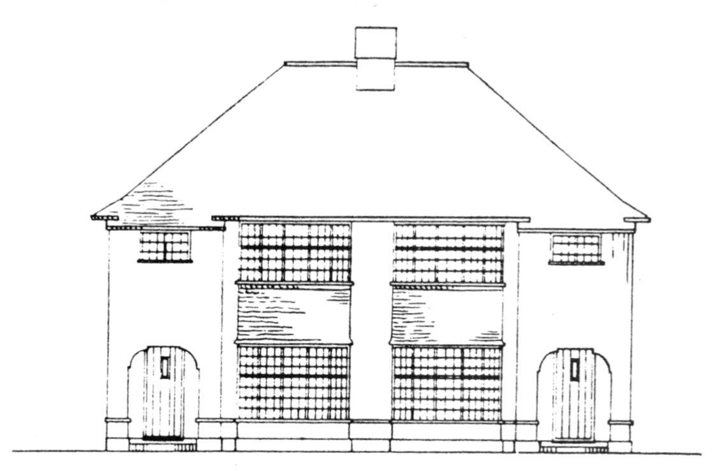

Well-built FREEHOLD houses containing 3 Bedrooms, 2 Reception Rooms, Bathroom (with closed-in bath and mixer fittings), Separate W.C., Large Kitchenette, Large Garden with space for Garage at rear, situate in the main Ruislip Road in the Borough of Ealing and standing about 120 feet above sea-level.

Buses to Ealing Broadway pass the Estate, and bus services to Oxford Circus, Wembley, London Bridge, Morden, etc., are within a few minutes' walk.

There is a good shopping centre close to the Estate.

Houses are wired for Electric Light, several Power points are installed, Gas points run to the principal fireplaces.

Ideal boiler fitted in Kitchenette; other fitments include Glass Fronted Cabinet, Draining Board and Gas Copper.

Floors of Bathroom and Kitchenette are covered with Marinite Jointless Flooring which obviates the necessity of Lino, and walls are partly tiled.

Tiled surrounds with Oak Mantels are fitted in Reception Rooms; Casement Doors lead from Dining-room to Garden; Mortice Locks fitted; Leaded Lights to all Front Rooms and Entrance Door.

Slate dampcourse; Cement Paths to Front Entrance and side and rear of house.

All rooms are airy with a maximum window space.

Roofs are covered with Trent Vale Tiles.

Close boarded fences are erected at rear, side, etc.

Purchase Price £795

No Road or Legal charges

Mortgage can be arranged. **£5 secures.**

For further particulars apply to:

A. E. GOODHEW, ***Builder and Contractor,***

Stanhope Estate, Ruislip Road, Greenford.

'Phone: Ealing 3084 Perivale 1223.

An estate agent's advert for houses on the Stanhope estate, 1933. The estate included Stanhope Park Road and Croyde Road (Avenue), which were built between 1930 and 1936 on the site of Stanhope Park House. Edward Otter, Sheriff of Middlesex from 1909 to 1910, had lived there. Stanhope Park itself had been built on the site of the former Stickleton Manor.

Greenford Road at the junction with Oldfield Lane North, *c.* 1939. The geography of the area changed in 1924 when Greenford Road was built, replacing Oldfield Lane as the principal north–south route. Greenford Road crossed Western Avenue, built in 1934, and Whitton Avenue West, which was being built during 1935. The Greenford flyover was not built until 1979.

Burwell Avenue, Greenford Green, *c.* 1940. Greenford Road was built by 1936, and speculative house building followed in the 1930s. By 1940 the area was largely built up, although a large open space survives on Horsenden Hill. The North Greenford estate, including Sherwood, Burwell and Ennismore Avenue, was built in the grounds of Greenford Place.

Sherwood Avenue, Greenford Green, was built by 1936, and is shown here in *c.* 1940. Shopping parades, The Oldfield superpub and Glaxo were built nearby on Greenford Road. The Glaxo factory, employing 2,000 people, opened in 1935 on a 20-acre site near the Grand Union Canal, and made infant foods and pharmaceutical products. It was designed by Wallis, Gilbert & partners, who designed the Hoover factory at Perivale from 1932. A school and church were opened on Horsenden Lane. The foundation stone for All Hallows, Horsenden Lane North, North Greenford, was laid by Lord Phillimore on 6 July 1940.

Ennismore Avenue, Greenford Green, 1940. The North Greenford estate provided a local source of workers for Glaxo in a similar way that the Perivale Park estate provided workers for the Hoover factory at Perivale. The estate was also served by good rail connections, with the Piccadilly Line being extended to Sudbury Hill in 1932, and the Great Western Railway's line to London, which became the Central Line in 1947.

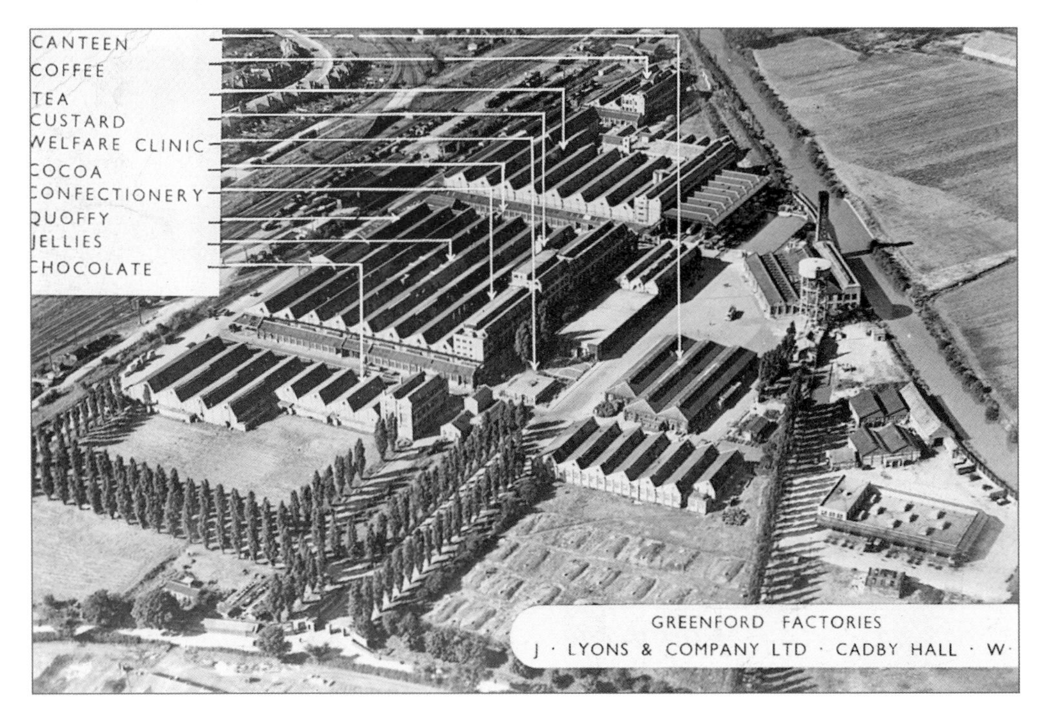

J. Lyons & Co. Factory, Oldfield Lane, Greenford, *c.* 1939. J. Lyons was opened in 1921, employing 2,000 workers for tea blending although it later manufactured chocolate, cocoa and confectionery. There were special railway sidings to the factory and the Grand Union Canal bordered the site. In 1958 a large new factory for making ice-cream was added to the works in Oldfield Lane.

J. Lyons & Co. Factory, Greenford, *c.* 1939. Hill Rise has been laid out with houses on the other side of the railway line. Lyons was not the only company to locate next to the canal. The Grand Union Canal with its capacity for the transportation of goods was important for industry and it drew factories to the area; these included Glaxo, Aladdin, and W.A. Bailey in 1900, the forerunner of the Rockware Glass Syndicate which made glass bottles.

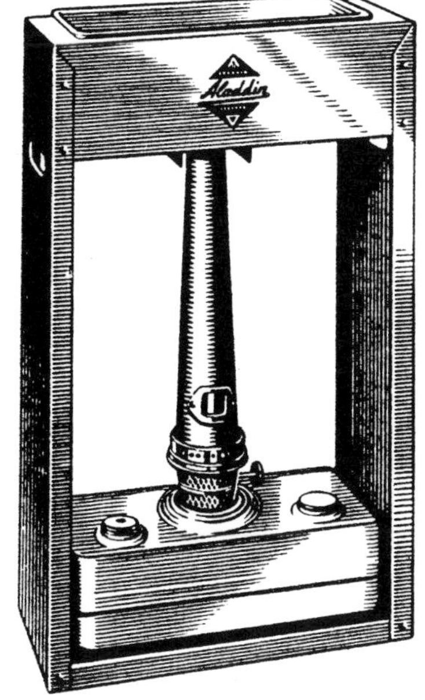

From Greenford to all parts of the world

Every week, in ever increasing numbers, Aladdin Lighting and Heating Units are shipped from Greenford to all parts of the world. It is this heavy demand from overseas that unavoidably restricts supplies to our Home Trade

The name the whole world knows

ALADDIN INDUSTRIES LTD., 55 ALADDIN BLDG., GREENFORD

Aladdin, Western Avenue, Greenford. Aladdin opened on Western Avenue in 1932, and manufactured lighting (lamps) and heating units. The factory had a central tower like an Italian campanile, designed by Nicholas & Dixon Spain.

Greenford station, January 1937. Greenford station was opened in 1904 on the Great Western Railway rail motor route from Westbourne Park, which explains the sign on the railings. The station approach was on the opposite side to the present station.

Greenford station on 20 December1954, advertising British Railways, Western Region and the Central Line. The station was designed by Brian Lewis, architect to the Great Western Railway until 1946. His designs were modified by Dr F.F. Curtis, the chief architect of British Rail (Western Region) in 1948 because of post-war shortages of materials. It was completed in 1949.

CENTRAL LINE EXTENSION

In June 1935 the government announced that the Central London tube line was to be extended at either end as part of the New Works Programme. It was renamed the Central Line in August 1937. Western Avenue had already opened up the area between North Acton and Greenford, the house building in the area aimed at those working in the factories. More growth was projected as the amount of traffic increased. Work on the railway began in 1937; the out-break of war two years later did not affect progress until June 1940, when building ceased. When work restarted in November 1946 only temporary stations were built at Hanger Lane, Perivale and Greenford because of a shortage of materials. Hanger Lane replaced Brentham and Park Royal West. The Central Line was opened from North Acton to Greenford on 30 June 1947 and from Greenford to West Ruislip on 21 November 1948. The war shortages meant that the projected extension to Denham was abandoned and the stations were down sized. The designs of Hanger Lane, Perivale and Greenford by Brian Lewis were modified by Dr F.F. Curtis to suit the limited range of materials available. As a result, Perivale lost a row of shops but the stations were still finished in 1949. Northolt did not have a permanent station building until 1961 because of restrictions on investment capital.

Greenford station, 6 April 1966. The parade of cars includes, from left to right: a Ford Zephyr, a Ford Prefect, a Ford Consul, a Mini van, a Morris Oxford Series VI Traveller, a Triumph Herald and a Sunbeam Rapier hardtop.

The Broadway, Ruislip Road, at the junction with Greenford Road, Greenford, *c.* 1960, with the Red Lion mock-Tudor pub on the corner and a no. 55 bus climbing the hill. There was an ale house in Greenford before 1692 but the Red Lion on Ruislip Road is first mentioned in 1726. After Greenford Road was built in 1924 the Red Lion was moved from the eastern corner of Windmill Lane and rebuilt on its present site in 1930. There were two cinemas in Greenford: the Odeon on Greenford Road, where Tescos now stands, and the Embassy on Ruislip Road, now demolished and rebuilt as the Central West office block.

Greenford Parade, Ruislip Road, *c.* 1965. The shopping parade was built on the site of Greenford Lodge. There were branches of several chain stores on The Broadway, including Burton's, the tailor of taste; J. Sainsburys; Boots, who opened in 1930; and Woolworths, who opened in 1931. Greenford Library was built in 1934 and Greenford school in 1937, by Middlesex County Council. Just out of view is the sports shop run by Steve Perryman, who played for and managed Brentford and Spurs.

PERIVALE

Perivale took its name from either 'Pear Valley' or 'Greenford Parva', which translates as Little or Small Greenford. It became part of Greenford Urban District Council in 1894. The population of Perivale was 55 in 1891, and the hamlet included the church, rectory, Church Farm and Grange Farm. A station was built in the fields by the Great Western Railway, and opened in 1904. In 1926 as part of Greenford UDC, Perivale was absorbed by Ealing. When Western Avenue was opened in 1929 factories relocated to Perivale. A. Sandersons moved from Chiswick and opened in the same year, making wallpaper in its factory on a 16-acre site on the other side of the railway before the famous Hoover factory was built between 1931 and 1935. The surrounding farmland was sold to housing developers and Perivale Park estate was built around the Hoover factory for the workers. Also, Sir Percy Bilton developed industrial units on the estate on Wadsworth Road. The site of Church Farm was developed as the Myllett Arms in 1935 and Grange Farm survived until 1939. The rectory was demolished in 1958, with only the church remaining today.

The Lych Gate, Perivale, in 1905, with the rectory on the left and on the right a notice from Greenford UDC dated May 1904, which warns that this is a footpath only. The Lych Gate with scissor-braced trusses dates from 1904 and was built in memory of Mrs Boosey from a bequest in her will.

Grand Junction Canal, Perivale. The narrow bridge was built in 1909 and carries Horsenden Lane North over the Paddington branch of the Grand Junction Canal, which opened in 1838. The road becomes a rural lane climbing up Horsenden Hill, which is 270 feet high. The same view today is obstructed by a footbridge and a pipe.

View from Horsenden Hill towards Ealing and Hanwell, *c.* 1914. The Grand Junction Canal is at the foot of the hill. Perivale station, opened in 1904, is on the embankment running across the photograph and the group of trees in the middle hides Perivale church beyond. Perivale Wood is on the right of the picture and beyond that, in the distance, is the Cuckoo Schools, Hanwell.

Perivale Bridge, *c.* 1911. The building on the left is a private house. The church behind was known as Perivale church until 1951 as it was believed to have no dedication. For a short time, 1931–51, it was labelled on maps as St James' Church. In 1951 a reference was found in the fifteenth-century will of Isabella Miles to 'the churchyard of St Mary of Little Greenford'. Since Perivale was also known as Greenford Parva, or Little Greenford, St Mary's was adopted as the new name for the church.

Perivale Bridge over the River Brent, *c.* 1911. On the bank opposite the church are cyclists, dog-walkers, walkers and a set of football posts. The path led to a rifle range, used by the Ealing Rifle Volunteers, which became part of the Ealing Golf Club from 1898. The bridge has been rebuilt recently.

The interior of Perivale church (St Mary's), *c.* 1911. The church was restored from 1868 by Robert Willey, who exposed the roof beams, and again by Laurence King in 1964, who also designed the new church of St Mary and St Nicholas, Perivale, in 1963. Of the two coloured windows in the nave, the one on the south wall is dedicated to Nathaniel Ravenor, formerly of Ravenor House, Greenford. Simon Coston donated the cover of the font in 1665. There is a monument by Sir Richard Westmacott to Ellen Nicholas, daughter of the headmaster of Great Ealing School.

Perivale church (St Mary's), shown here in *c.* 1911, was founded in AD 1135 and has a thirteenth-century nave, a fifteenth-century roof and a sixteenth-century weatherboarded tower. It was reputed to be the smallest church in Middlesex. When the A40 was built, the church was cut off from the new estates on the other side of the road and a new church of St Mary and St Nicholas was opened in a hut on Devon Road in 1934. The hut was replaced by a dual-purpose hall on Federal Road in 1935, which became the location of the new church consecrated in 1965. In 1972 St Mary's, Perivale, was closed. After several instances of vandalism, in 1976 a charitable trust was formed to look after St Mary's and to raise money for it. In 1981 it became the West London Arts Centre, established by the Friends of St Mary's.

Perivale Rectory, *c*. 1904. Built to the north of the church in the fifteenth century, the rectory began life as a half-timbered building. The south wing was added in 1699. The rectory was demolished in 1958 and a modern house has been built in the grounds.

Perivale Rectory, *c*. 1904. The churchyard was popular with middle-class Londoners as a cemetery until 1906. At this time, the people's warden took legal action against the rector to stop the burial of non-parishioners and won. A later rector helped to name the Myllett Arms, which opened nearby on Western Avenue in 1935. He suggested that it ought to be named after the Millet family, who bought the manor of Perivale in 1573 and owned Hanwell Park during the sixteenth and seventeenth centuries.

The Hoover Building, Western Avenue, Perivale, *c.* 1935. In 1931 a duty was put on British imports – up to this time Hoovers were imported from America. This and the setting up of a National Grid in 1933 encouraged Hoover to open a factory in Britain. It even brought 60 Canadian Hoover workers to Britain to be part of the 600-strong workforce. When Western Avenue cut through Perivale in 1929, Hoover followed Sandersons and built a factory on an 8-acre site off the thoroughfare. It was completed between 1931 and 1935 and is shown here before the canteen was built. The white fascia was designed in the Art Deco style by Wallis, Gilbert & partners, who later built the Glaxo factory at Greenford in 1935. The Hoover Building contained the offices and the factory, which made Hoover carpet cleaners. Three thousand people from the area including Ealing, Perivale and Greenford were employed there. Percy Marshall from Greenford worked for Hoover for the best part of twenty-five years. The factory closed in 1982 and remained unoccupied until 1991, when Tescos took it over and illuminated it in green lighting. The road was moved back for road widening in the 1980s and with it the Art Deco Egyptian gatepiers and railings.

The Hoover Building, *c.* 1935. The white symmetrical glazed front was typical of the thirties and provided a white facade against which the green corporate logo, the Art Deco Egyptian motif and the coloured lining stood out. The Southern Railway used this style for its stations. At each end were recessed stair towers with quadrant-shaped corner windows with green glazing bars. The motif over the main entrance is reminiscent of an Egyptian fan-tail, joined to an American Indian step design with echoes of an Aztec temple. The coloured lining of black, blue, green, gold and especially orange show the influence of the Russian ballet. Egyptian and Aztec art forms as well as the Russian ballet were all major influences on Art Deco style (see p. 1).

The bus and coach passenger shelter in front of a row of shops on Teignmouth Gardens, Western Avenue, Perivale, February 1935. The row of shops was built at the same time as the Hoover Building to the east of it, and the foundations of the bank, which completed the row, are visible on the right. The row of shop fronts was appropriately clad in glazed tiles with green trimmings. E. Cash stores (no. 6) is now an off-licence, Breakell's (no. 5) is now Devine Creations, a unisex hairdresser, and no. 4 is now Terry's News.

The canteen was added in 1938, by architect J. MacGregor, to the west of the Hoover Building. It was also glazed in white, but was a steel-framed construction, not reinforced concrete like the main building. The ribbon windows contrast with the angular vertical window of the staircase. The canteen was not just a place for eating; it also had a dance floor and a theatre at one end.

The Hoover Building and the canteen. Traffic lights have now been set up on Western Avenue. The canteen building is now being developed by Kyle Stewart as offices.

The Hoover Building Medical Room, Western Avenue, *c.* 1938. The building indicates Hoover's commitment to its employees as it was built before the days of the National Health Service when every visit to the doctor had to be paid for.

Rydal Crescent, Perivale, *c.* 1935. Hoover encouraged the building of the Perivale Park estate, which was built around the factory for its workers. On the estate Cliffords built houses on Thames and Calder Avenues and HEC built houses on Bilton Road. Shops were built on Bilton Road and Ealing Council built a school in 1934 and a library by 1935. A large pub, the Myllett Arms, designed by E.B. Musman, was built in 1935 almost opposite the factory. Churches were opened on Federal Road in 1935 and on Medway Drive in 1936. Sir Percy Bilton developed commercial and industrial property along Bilton Road and Wadsworth Road, including Philco Radio and Pond's. Sir Percy Bilton is commemorated today by Bilton House on Uxbridge Road, Ealing, built in the 1960s.

Perivale station, Horsenden Lane South, January 1937. It was opened in 1904 by the Great Western Railway as a wooden halt with pagoda huts on the opposite side of the road to where the station is today. The sign points the way to Cliffords' Perivale Park estate where houses were being offered for £595 and £725, the latter on Thames and Calder Avenues. Houses have already been built on the other side of the bridge. Only forty houses remained in November 1935 on the six-month-old Perivale Wood estate, described as 'isolated from other estates' and 'rural, yet only 5 miles from marble Arch'. The 90-acre Perivale Park Golf Course was opened in 1934.

Perivale station, 29 December 1954. The new station on Horsenden Lane was opened in 1949 to the east of the old halt. Because of the financial constraints of the early post-war years a single storey southward extension of shops was never built.

TWYFORD

Twyford became a civil parish in 1857, and in 1894 joined with Great Greenford and Perivale to become Greenford Urban District. In about 1807 Thomas Willan, a dairy farmer who had the lease of the land which became Regents Park, had bought the manor house and employed William Atkinson to turn it into a romantic castellated abbey. Willan also built Twyford Abbey Farm for the principal tenant. Willan's daughter, Isabella Douglas-Willan, inherited the Twyford Abbey estate in 1828 on the death of her father. She divided the estate into three parts, keeping one part for herself and living in one of the lodges on it. The other lodge was on Hanger Lane. In 1901 a 102-acre site on a 117-year lease at Twyford was selected to be the permanent showground for the Royal Agricultural Society under the name Park Royal. In 1903 Park Royal and Twyford Abbey station was built to serve it. However, the scheme was not a success and was abandoned in 1905. During the First World War the area provided a different service, helping to meet the demand for munitions factories. The North Circular was built through the area in 1926 at the same time as Twyford became part of the Municipal Borough of Ealing. In 1934 it was transferred to Willesden but after public protest it was returned to Ealing. The Guinness factory was built on the site of the munitions factories in 1936.

The lodge at the entrance to Twyford Abbey Drive off Twyford Abbey Road, *c.* 1908. Twyford Abbey is hidden by the trees behind the lodge. The drive was private until 1930 when Ealing Borough Council took over its repair. The lodge was rebuilt and extended in 1935 when the parapets and the ivy were removed; in 1964 the chimney pots were removed and the windows replaced.

Twyford Abbey, *c.* 1910. The estate was bought by the Roman Catholic Alexian Brothers in 1902, who enlarged the abbey as a convalescent home for retired gentlemen from 1905. They tried to use the old parish church of St Mary's as a chapel but in 1907 this was restored for Anglican worship. The monks sold off land around the estate, for example Twyford Bridge Farm to Guinness in 1940, and continued enlarging the abbey until 1962. In 1958 a new church was built, which incorporated the old one as a Lady Chapel. In 1988 the retirement home was closed but the abbey is still owned by the Alexian Brothers today.

Park Royal and Twyford Abbey station in 1922. The station had been opened by the Great Western Railway on 23 June 1903 to serve the Royal Agricultural Showground immediately to the east. The station consisted of a simple corrugated-iron shack on the up-side, reached by a flight of steps from Twyford Abbey Road below. In 1907 it became part of the District Line of the Underground Group. The station was renamed Park Royal and relocated on Western Avenue in 1931 when the Piccadilly Line was extended.

Royal Agricultural Showground main entrance, as it was during the period 1901 to 1905.

Royal Agricultural Showgrounds, 1901–5. Sutton Seeds and other agricultural companies have trade stands, but there are very few people to be seen. Although Park Royal and Twyford Abbey station opened on 23 June 1903, the opening day of the show, it failed to boost crowds. People considered it to be too far out from the centre of London. After the lowest attendance for twenty-eight years and another poor two years, the site was abandoned in 1905.

Royal Agricultural Showgrounds, 1901–5. Park Royal was still a rural area as the North Circular was not built until 1926 and Western Avenue not until 1929. Factories then filled in many of the areas in between.

Royal Agricultural Show horse ground, 1901–5. Shire horses are being judged in the horse ring. It was reputed to hold up to 40,000 spectators and was used by Queens Park Rangers Football Club from 1904 to 1907 until the club moved a few hundred yards to a larger ground built by the Great Western Railway.

Munitions factory, Abbey Road, 1914–18. After the out-break of the First World War the army took over Park Royal and the showgrounds in February 1915, and Queens Park Rangers were homeless again. During the First World War munitions factories were built off Abbey Road, Park Royal. The Guinness factory was built on the site of the munitions factories in 1936. Park Royal Bodies for Buses was one industry which took its name from the site.

Four Haymills Estates

ON THE

UNDERGROUND

Hendon Heights
Hendon Central
N.W.4

Barn Hill
Wembley Park
Middlesex

Shirehall Park
Golders Green
N.W.4

Hanger Hill
Ealing, W.5

Haymills House, Type E
Contains Lounge Hall, 2 Reception and 4 Bedrooms, Kitchen, Tiled Scullery and Bathroom. From £1,525 Leasehold and £1,675 Freehold. (Barn Hill Estate prices.)

Every house has Space for Garage or Garage

Haymills Houses are planned on the most modern labour-saving principles, and are of various types, containing 3, 4 or 5 bedrooms, with 2 or 3 reception rooms. Decorations to purchaser's selection. Liberal advances are made by the Cheshunt Building Society on all Haymills Houses.

There is a Haymills House for every need and purse

Write, 'phone or call, for Illustrated Booklet of the Estate in which you are interested. Haymills Ltd. have offices on each estate, and representatives in constant attendance, including Saturdays and Sundays.

HAYMILLS LIMITED

**Head Office (Dept. D), 1 Grand Parade,
Forty Lane, Wembley Park, Middlesex**

Telephone: Wembley 1736 (3 lines)

An estate agent's advert for Haymills' houses on Hanger Hill, 1933.

Park Royal (Hanger Hill) station, July 1936. It replaced Park Royal and Twyford Abbey station on Twyford Abbey Road, which had opened in 1903. It was resited on Western Avenue on 6 July 1931 as part of the Piccadilly Line extension of Park Royal. It was renamed Park Royal (Hanger Hill) on 1 March 1936. The station building was designed by Welch and Lander as part of their development at Hanger Hill. The bus is on General route 79 from Park Royal to North Wembley, weekdays only.

Park Royal (Hanger Hill) station, July 1936. It was rebuilt to serve the Hanger Hill estate, built by Haymills Ltd with the architects Welch, Cachemaille-Day and Lander. A series of concentric crescents was laid out on a former golf course between 1928 and 1932. Haymills Ltd also built the railway depot at Ruislip. The Haymills Houses office is in the centre and on the right is the site of a super service station for Campbell Symonds & Co. Empire Garages.

Hanger Lane station during May 1950 when traffic lights were added. It replaced Brentham and Park Royal West stations, which closed in 1947 as part of the Central Line extension. The temporary street level building at Hanger Lane was replaced by a circular entrance hall and ticket offices on 2 January 1949. The station is now at the heart of the Hanger Lane gyratory traffic system and Share Staff Recruitment occupies shops at the side. Stowell's Corner thirties office and shop development is opposite.

A 1955 advert for Chain of Ealing, with a man shown reading the advert on the tube.

NORTHOLT

For much of its history the borough was known as Northall, complementing its neighbour Southall. The tiny fourteenth-century church of St Mary the Virgin overlooks the remains of the green. The old drum pump was installed by public subscription in 1873, opposite the church on Northolt Green. The arrival of the Paddington Canal to Northolt in 1801 allowed hay to be grown profitably for London instead of wheat. The canal also allowed the local brick earth to be transported cheaply, and by the end of the century the New Patent Brick Company occupied 36 acres by the canal. Although a railway station was built at Northolt in 1907, sales of farms and their development by speculators did not start until the 1920s. The building of Western Avenue in 1934 east–west across the centre set the pattern for further building. Northolt aerodrome, situated just outside the borough boundary, opened in 1915 and was used as an airfield during the Second World War. At the end of 1949, 8,654 families who had been bombed out in Ealing were awaiting accommodation, and to solve the problem the council bought the racecourse at Northolt Park in 1950 and developed the racecourse estate for housing. People moved out there from Ealing especially after the Central Line extension was built in 1948.

With best wishes from Northolt.

A General bus on route 140 to Colindale at the bus shelter on Petts Hill, next to the racecourse at Northolt Park in January 1935. The station had opened in 1926 as South Harrow and Roxeth station but was renamed Northolt Park in 1929 when the pony-racing track opened. Race meetings were held until 1950, when the council bought the track and built the Racecourse housing estate on the land.

A bus shelter on Petts Hill at Northolt Park. The pub, offering Watneys Ales and Reids Stout, opened in 1929 and is now called The Oast House. The advert on the left is for New Ideal Homesteads, and the path led to Northolt Park station on the line between Denham and Marylebone, which was operated by the London and North Eastern Railway.

Northolt Halt, seen here in January 1937, was opened in 1907 by the Great Western Railway. Wymans, a local stationer's, has an outlet in the kiosk on the right, and maintained its presence in the new station opened in 1948. The telephone box is a type K3, first introduced in 1929. The concrete K3 was used throughout the United Kingdom on both urban and rural sites. The usual livery was cream stipple paint and red glazing bars. Around 12,000 units were built all over the country during the six years between 1929 and 1935.

Northolt Halt, January 1937. Percival Smirk houses on Western Avenue, Northolt, are being advertised for £595. The houses under construction on the left are on Cranleigh Gardens.

SEE THE MAGNIFICENT

FREEHOLD BUNGALOWS

At NORTHOLT MANOR

STATELY DWELLINGS AT A LOW PRICE

On the Northolt Manor Estate, Two Types of Bungalows are in course of erection. Type A, as illustrated, is Priced at

£600 FREEHOLD

Average size of Plots, 110 feet by 30 feet.

Two DOUBLE BEDROOMS, One LARGE RECEPTION ROOM, KITCHEN and BATHROOM. There is also room for Garage.

Sturdily Built with Best Materials. Nine inch Outer Brick Walls and four-and-half inch Interior Brick Walls are one of the outstanding Standardisations. DOUBLE SLATE DAMP COURSE and BOARDED ROOFS under tiles are Standard. Leaded Light Windows and French Windows to Garden from the Reception Rooms.

Other Features include:—

Enamel "Ideal" boiler. Nickel-plated taps in kitchen and bathroom. Coal Shed. Spring fencing. Cement rear court. Light fittings to lamp holders. "Easiwork" type dresser (standard fittings). Tiled floors in hall, kitchen, and bathroom.

There are No ROAD CHARGES. CONCRETE ROADS ARE ALREADY LAID DOWN. There are No LEGAL, MORTGAGE, SURVEY, or STAMPING EXPENSES. Decorations are to the purchaser's own choice.

THE COST. The repayments to the Building Society work out as follows:— **17s. 6d. weekly. The Rates are approximately 4s. 10d. weekly, including Water.**

EXCELLENT TRAINS. There is an excellent service of trains, Paddington being reached within twenty minutes. There are extra trains during the rush hours. Cheap day returns are issued to Paddington for 11d., and a weekly ticket costs 5s. 2d.

Furnished Show Bungalow on Estate, viz. 14, Manor Avenue. Telephone, PERIVALE 1878. Representative always in attendance.

A. J. BOND, *Builder*,

7, Church Avenue, Northolt, Middlesex.

Telephone: PERIVALE 2184.

An estate agent's advert for the Northolt Manor estate, 1933. Bungalows are for sale for £600 on Manor Avenue, built by A.J. Bond. In 1905 Frank Grace was the farmer at Manor Farm. In 1927 the farm was purchased by Frank Archibald Wright, a Hanwell butcher who launched an unsuccessful scheme to make a Garden City at Northolt, but by 1934 A.J. Bond was developing the land.

NORTHOLT

NORTHOLT IS HIGH AND HEALTHY.

The fame of The Super Kitchen Houses at Northolt is spreading far and wide. It is an accepted fact and admitted by all our purchasers that our houses are the cheapest and best in the district.

£595 Freehold. Total Deposit £30.

REPAYMENTS ...	18/10	per week
RATES	3/3	" "
TOTAL REPAYMENTS	22/1	" "

£675 Freehold. Total Deposit £35.

REPAYMENTS ...	21/-	per week
RATES	4/-	" "
TOTAL REPAYMENTS	25/-	"

ACCOMMODATION.—Large Entrance Hall with Coloured Leaded Lights in Windows. 2 Large Reception Rooms fitted with Super Tile Surrounds, and Oak and Mahogany Mantels. Bay Windows in Each Room. Tiled Kitchen, 12 feet long, containing up-to-date Kitchen Cabinet, "Ideal" Boiler, Gas Copper, Deep Sink and Draining Board.
3 Large Bedrooms with Bay Window in Each Room, 2 being fitted with Tile Surrounds of the latest pattern and Coal Fireplaces.
Tiled Bathroom containing White Porcelain Enamel English Square Enclosed Bath with Chromium Plated Fittings, including Hot and Cold Mixer and Shower. China Lavatory Basin.
Separate Tiled Lavatory.
There are Large Gardens both front and rear, and Space for Garage for all Houses.

No Road Charges. No Legal Costs. No Survey Fees. No Stamp Duties.

TRAVELLING FACILITIES.—Northolt Park, L.N.E.R. Station adjoins the Estate from which Marylebone can be reached in 23 minutes by all trains. Cheap Season Tickets are available.
South Harrow District and Piccadilly Tube Station is but 8 minutes' walk from the Estate, and fast through trains are available to all parts of the City and West End.
Bus No. 114D passes the end of the Road.

ROBERTS Estate Office,

BYRON 1366. "Lagonda," Petts Hill, Northolt, Middx.

Estate Office OPEN EVERY DAY

An estate agent's advert for houses on Petts Hill, Northolt, 1933.

The Crown pub on The Green, Northolt, *c.* 1930, after it was rebuilt in 1925. It was altered again in 1976. The Crown is first mentioned in 1715 in the parish records and was licensed by 1746. In 1830 the tenant also ran a public slaughter house, and between 1829 and 1834 the manor court was sometimes held at the inn. In 1939 the 2nd London Irish rifles were stationed at Northolt, guarding vulnerable points such as Northolt aerodrome.

Northolt station, 6 April 1966. The halt was rebuilt as Northolt station in 1948 when the Central Line was extended from Greenford to Ruislip along the Great Western Railway route. The permanent station building designed by British Rail architects Curtis and Cavanagh was not finished until November 1961 because of capital investment restrictions. Wymans' kiosk is visible, as is J. Leon's, the tobacconist's, who also had a shop at Perivale station.

FURTHER READING

Books consulted include Charles Jones's *Ealing from Village to Corporate Town* (1902), C.M. Neaves's *History of Greater Ealing* (1931), and F. Green and S. Wolff's *London and Suburbs Old and New* (1933).

Books published in the 1980s and 1990s include M. Gooding's *Ealing in the 1930s & '40s* (1985), B. Cherry and N. Pevsner's *Buildings of England: London 3, Northwest* (1991), Peter Hounsell's *Ealing and Hanwell Past* (1991), Pamela D. Edwards' *Ealing and Acton in Old Picture Postcards* (1993), M. Gooding's *Ealing As It Was* (1993) and *Environs of Ealing in Old Photographs* (1995), and Richard Essen's *Ealing and Northfields in Old Photographs* (1996).

ACKNOWLEDGEMENTS

Thanks are due to the following for the use of pictures: Hugh Robertson at the London Transport Museum: front cover, p. 33 lower, p. 35 lower, p. 76 upper, p. 77 upper and lower, p. 84 lower, pp. 98–9, p. 102 upper, p. 106 lower, p. 107 lower, p. 110, p. 117, p. 118, pp. 120–1, p. 124 upper; and the National Monuments Record: p. 1, p. 107 upper, p. 108 upper, p. 109 upper.

INDEX

BRITAIN IN OLD PHOTOGRAPHS

Aberystwyth & North Ceredigion
Around Abingdon
Acton
Alderney: A Second Selection
Along the Avon from Stratford to Tewkesbury
Altrincham
Amersham
Around Amesbury
Anglesey
Arnold & Bestwood
Arnold & Bestwood: A Second Selection
Arundel & the Arun Valley
Ashbourne
Around Ashby-de-la-Zouch
Avro Aircraft
Aylesbury
Balham & Tooting
Banburyshire
Barnes, Mortlake & Sheen
Barnsley
Bath
Beaconsfield
Bedford
Bedfordshire at Work
Bedworth
Beverley
Bexley
Bideford
Bilston
Birmingham Railways
Bishop's Stortford & Sawbridgeworth
Bishopstone & Seaford
Bishopstone & Seaford: A Second Selection
Black Country Aviation
Black Country Railways
Black Country Road Transport
Blackburn
Blackpool
Around Blandford Forum
Bletchley
Bolton
Bournemouth
Bradford
Braintree & Bocking at Work
Brecon
Brentwood
Bridgwater & the River Parrett
Bridlington
Bridport & the Bride Valley
Brierley Hill
Brighton & Hove
Brighton & Hove: A Second Selection
Bristol
Around Bristol
Brixton & Norwood
Early Broadstairs & St Peters
Bromley, Keston & Hayes

Buckingham & District
Burford
Bury
Bushbury
Camberwell
Cambridge
Cannock Yesterday & Today
Canterbury: A Second Selection
Castle Combe to Malmesbury
Chadwell Heath
Chard & Ilminster
Chatham Dockyard
Chatham & Gillingham
Cheadle
Cheam & Belmont
Chelmsford
Cheltenham: A Second Selection
Cheltenham at War
Cheltenham in the 1950s
Chepstow & the River Wye
Chesham Yesterday & Today
Cheshire Railways
Chester
Chippenham & Lacock
Chiswick
Chorley & District
Cirencester
Around Cirencester
Clacton-on-Sea
Around Clitheroe
Clwyd Railways
Clydesdale
Colchester
Colchester 1940–70
Colyton & Seaton
The Cornish Coast
Corsham & Box
The North Cotswolds
Coventry: A Second Selection
Around Coventry
Cowes & East Cowes
Crawley New Town
Around Crawley
Crewkerne & the Ham Stone Villages
Cromer
Croydon
Crystal Palace, Penge & Anerley
Darlington
Darlington: A Second Selection
Dawlish & Teignmouth
Deal
Derby
Around Devizes
Devon Aerodromes
East Devon at War
Around Didcot & the Hagbournes
Dorchester
Douglas
Dumfries
Dundee at Work
Durham People

Durham at Work
Ealing & Northfields
East Grinstead
East Ham
Eastbourne
Elgin
Eltham
Ely
Enfield
Around Epsom
Esher
Evesham to Bredon
Exeter
Exmouth & Budleigh Salterton
Fairey Aircraft
Falmouth
Farnborough
Farnham: A Second Selection
Fleetwood
Folkestone: A Second Selection
Folkestone: A Third Selection
The Forest of Dean
Frome
Fulham
Galashiels
Garsington
Around Garstang
Around Gillingham
Gloucester
Gloucester: from the Walwin Collection
North Gloucestershire at War
South Gloucestershire at War
Gosport
Goudhurst to Tenterden
Grantham
Gravesend
Around Gravesham
Around Grays
Great Yarmouth
Great Yarmouth: A Second Selection
Greenwich & Woolwich
Grimsby
Around Grimsby
Grimsby Docks
Gwynedd Railways
Hackney: A Second Selection
Hackney: A Third Selection
From Haldon to Mid-Dartmoor
Hammersmith & Shepherds Bush
Hampstead to Primrose Hill
Harrow & Pinner
Hastings
Hastings: A Second Selection
Haverfordwest
Hayes & West Drayton
Around Haywards Heath
Around Heathfield
Around Heathfield: A Second Selection
Around Helston

Around Henley-on-Thames
Herefordshire
Herne Bay
Heywood
The High Weald
The High Weald: A Second Selection
Around Highworth
Around Highworth & Faringdon
Hitchin
Holderness
Honiton & the Otter Valley
Horsham & District
Houghton-le-Spring & Hetton-le-Hole
Houghton-le-Spring & Hetton-le-Hole: A Second Selection
Huddersfield: A Second Selection
Huddersfield: A Third Selection
Ilford
Ilfracombe
Ipswich: A Second Selection
Islington
Jersey: A Third Selection
Kendal
Kensington & Chelsea
East Kent at War
Keswick & the Central Lakes
Around Keynsham & Saltford
The Changing Face of Keynsham
Kingsbridge
Kingston
Kinver
Kirkby & District
Kirkby Lonsdale
Around Kirkham
Knowle & Dorridge
The Lake Counties at Work
Lancashire
The Lancashire Coast
Lancashire North of the Sands
Lancashire Railways
East Lancashire at War
Around Lancaster
Lancing & Sompting
Around Leamington Spa
Around Leamington Spa: A Second Selection
Leeds in the News
Leeds Road & Rail
Around Leek
Leicester
The Changing Face of Leicester
Leicester at Work
Leicestershire People
Around Leighton Buzzard & Linslade
Letchworth
Lewes
Lewisham & Deptford: A Second Selection
Lichfield